The Way I See It

Dueling Interpretations
of
American History

The Way I See It

Dueling Interpretations
of
American History

Edited By

Jason L. Hanson
University of Colorado

Brandywine Press • Maplecrest, NY

Table of Contents

Introduction

Telling Stories

My grandfather, like many grandparents, knows how to tell a good story. His favorite stories (and mine too) recall growing up on the prairie in tiny Hendricks, Minnesota, during the 1930s and '40s—duck hunting before school for that night's dinner, rigging a sheet to sail down the frozen lake on ice skates, pitching hay from dawn to dark, backing the tractor up against the door of an occupied outhouse, playing offense, defense, and halftime trombone at high school football games. A good dinner spent with him will bring out some of these stories, and a good fishing trip often nets more stories than fish.

From these stories, sometimes repeated but never tiresome, I learned not only about where my grandfather came from but also about storytelling. In a good, well-constructed story, the beginning usually governs where the tale will end, and the end point often determines what the story means. When my grandfather tells me about going out before school to hunt ducks, the story ends with what the family had for dinner that evening, but its significance has more to do with a way of remembering his past than with how good a shot he was. Of such stories—the everyday as well as the extraordinary—are our lives and our history made, and it is the job of historians to synthesize and interpret them. Just as my grandfather has converted the most important parts of his identity into a roster of stories that help him understand what his life has meant and how it fits into the larger narratives of history, so too have Americans drawn a sense of national identity from the stories of our past.

Fourteen of our nation's stories are collected in this book. Each story is drawn from a different period in American history, from the time Indians first appeared on the continent to the twenty-first-century War on Terror, and each resonates with significance for the nation today. Every topic in this book has provoked passionate debate between observers at the time and among generations of historians who followed. Their meaning is unsettled. Contrary to how it is sometimes presented, the development of the American past was not a sequence of neat and tidy events with meanings agreed upon at the time and logically built upon one another. Rather, it was—and remains to this day—a discordant tangle of ongoing debate and interpretation. This book presents some of those debates, some in the words of the historical figures who participated in them, some in the voices of modern historians who have studied them. In every case, there are at least two sides to the story and multiple possible meanings.

Each chapter focuses on one of these debates. After a brief introduction to the period and the issue at hand, two dueling interpretations of the topic present different ways (but not necessarily the only ways) of understanding it. Finally, some questions are outlined to help center attention on essential points and spark discussion. My hope is that these discussions will not only cover the chapter's main topic but also raise some of the more provocative broader questions that make the study of history so compelling. Questions like:

- What points of contingency, places where things might have gone differently, exist in the American story? Was the defeat of the Indians inevitable? What if women had been enfranchised with black men? Was the Dust Bowl avoidable?

- What continuities bridge past and present? Why do the colonists' reasons for developing a system of black slavery matter today? Should the disagreements over the Constitution voiced by the nation's founders be considered in modern debates over their original intent? Can we learn anything from the Holocaust that will prevent future genocides?

- What if people in our history books were as complex and conflicted as people are today? Was Lincoln really as heroic as we make him out to be (and does he need to be)? Were murdered missionaries martyrs or villains, or something of both?

- What role do (or should) historians assume in society? Should they offer judgments about the past, or just seek to understand how and why it unfolded the way it did? Can we apply lessons from the past to our experiences in the present?

The answers that each reader gives to these questions will help to determine the meaning that each draws from these stories. Like my grandfather, we are all building our own catalogs of meaningful stories to help us understand how we became the people and the nation we are today.

Despite what it says on the cover, no one puts together a book like this alone, and I have many people to thank for their help in putting together this one. Patty Limerick indirectly set this project in motion and, in concert with a long line of excellent teachers, helped me develop the skills it required. David Burner guided it from the beginning and helped me through each stage. Tom West injected new ideas and energy exactly when they were needed most, and has been indefatigable in his efforts to improve it. My colleagues at the University of Colorado History Department and the Center of the American West offered their expertise freely, and numerous good friends and family have shared their thoughts, their dinner tables, and everything in between as it was needed. The people at Brandywine Press, especially Renzo Melaragno, did more than I'll ever know to make a reality of the book in my head. My parents and grandparents taught me things more important than anything I ever learned from a book, and their love and support is reflected on these pages. And Stacie, especially, contributed to this project in every sense of the word: With her sharp eyes, indulgent patience, and never-ending encouragement she made this a better book. Anyone working with such stellar collaborators is lucky indeed, and any errors that remain on these pages should be counted against me alone.

My deepest gratitude goes to the men and women who devoted their lives to making this a nation worth writing about and striving to understand. Their debates arise from their passion to change the world around them for the better, and whether or not we agree with their interpretation, we can all be inspired by their example. Finally, my apologies go to Jon Stewart, whom I count among their number.

1
Origin Stories
Where Did American Indians Come From?

Modern science traces American Indians to ancestors who migrated from Asia to North America on a now-submerged land bridge across the Bering Strait between ten and twenty-five thousand years ago. In the excerpts below, Colin Calloway surveys the kaleidoscope of origin stories surrounding the Indian presence in North America, from tribal traditions to prevailing scientific theory. Without discounting the value of tribal origin stories, which may code historical knowledge in metaphor, he presents the strong evidence supporting the Bering Strait migration theory (as well as some provocative and complicating recent evidence from South American discoveries). Historian Vine Deloria, Jr., a Sioux Indian, rejects the notion that the ancestors of America's tribes arrived via the land bridge, lambasting scientists who "just seem to make it up as they go along." He details objections to the theory and makes clear the modern cultural stakes of this historical debate.

Although the disputes surrounding the Bering Strait theory challenge it on archeological and scientific grounds, the heart of the controversy involves the political and cultural questions it raises. Some American Indian scholars and political activists—Vine Deloria, Jr., was both—assail the theory as an effort by Americans of European ancestry to portray Indians as relative latecomers to the continent, just another immigrant group not so different from any other group of people in North America. According to this interpretation, the Bering Strait theory is a way of denying the special relationship to the land claimed by Indian people, an attempt to avoid admitting that non-Indians were (and are) recent intruders. Some go further and challenge the arrogance of EuroAmerican science in setting its authority above that of the origin stories that numerous tribal groups still treasure.

Participants on both sides of the debate agree on the difficulty of knowing with any certainty what actually happened so deep in the past. They diverge over the question of how to best approach what can be known. Some trust in the authority of their cultural traditions, while others place their faith in the discoveries of honest scientific inquiry. How does a diligent historian reconcile these two perspectives with cultural sensitivity and an appropriate regard for science?

Origins and Emergences
Colin G. Calloway

Falling water levels during the Ice Age exposed a huge area of land across what is now the Bering Strait. According to the "most likely opinion," people moved across it from Asia. As the continental glaciers retreated, an ice-free corridor developed between the Laurentide and Cordilleran ice sheets, opening a passage between interior Alaska and the rest of North America through which people are believed to have migrated and in subsequent millennia fanned out to fill the Americas. People may have come in phases, perhaps some twenty to twenty-five thousand years ago and again between ten and fourteen thousand years ago, with glaciers blocking migration during the last ice age about twelve or fourteen thousand years ago.

D'Arcy McNickle portrayed the Beringian migration as an epic human drama and an Ice Age tale of discovery. McNickle was an enrolled member of the Flathead tribe. After a stint at the Chemawa boarding school in Oregon, he sold his land allotment to finance his studies at Oxford University, returned to the United States, and worked as a BIA [Bureau of Indian Affairs] official implementing John Collier's Indian New Deal in the 1930s. He was a founding member of the National Congress of American Indians and the founding director of the Center for the History of the American Indian at the Newberry Library in Chicago, which was renamed in his honor after his death in 1977. He was also a novelist and historian and a gifted storyteller. "The world was full of rumors just then, a marvelous thing

From Colin G. Calloway, *One Vast Winter Count: The Native American West Before Lewis and Clark* (Lincoln: University of Nebraska Press, 2003), 27-32. Reprinted with permission.

had happened: a new land had been discovered, and just when it was needed. The people had wandered to the end of the world, in quest of food and safety." The rumors told of a new land where meat was plentiful and life was easy. "The older people, sitting in their crudely made tents of skin, their eyes blinded by smoke and snow-gazing, were inclined to shrug their shoulders. They had heard of such things before." But the young people would not be put off. Pushed by hunger, they drifted on. "Like sand in an hourglass, pouring grain by grain. Over many thousands of years, wandering bands of people drifted toward the end of one world and crossed over into another."

Kiowa author N. Scott Momaday also related the standard line that the ancestors of Indian people came from Asia by means of Beringia, then pushed south through a corridor between ice sheets and dispersed across the Americas over the next seven thousand years. Yet Momaday knows other, Kiowa stories of the peopling of America: "The Kiowas came one by one into this world through a hollow log. There were many more than now, but not all of them got out. There was a woman whose body was swollen up with child, and she got stuck in the log. After that, no one could get through, and that is why the Kiowas are a small tribe in number. . . . They called themselves *Kwuda*, 'coming out.'"

The peoples who pioneered the West had their own stories of how it, and they, came into existence. Some peoples had priests who "recited memorized liturgies recounting tribal origins"; others had multiple accounts of the origins of the world. A century ago, Tawakoni Jim told anthropologist George A. Dorsey the Wichitas' story of the creation: "When the earth was created it was composed of land and water, but they were not yet separated. The land was floating on the water, and darkness was everywhere." Man Never Known on Earth (Kinnekeasus) was the only man that existed, and he created all things. He made a man whose name was Having Power to Carry Light (Kiarsidia) and a woman named Bright Shining Woman (Kashatski-hakatidise). "After the man and the woman were made they dreamed that things were made for them and when they woke they had the things of which they had dreamed." Having Power to Carry Light traveled east to a grass lodge, where he found light. New villages sprang up; there were more people, but the people "knew neither where they had come from nor how to live." Having Power to Carry Light and Bright Shining Woman went from village to village, teaching the inhabitants how to use the things they had. Having Power to Carry Light taught the men to make bows and arrows and to hunt, then disappeared to become the early morning star. Bright Shining Woman showed the women how to plant and raise corn, then disappeared into the sky and became the moon.

Pawnees on the east-central plains said they came from the stars and would return to them. According to Pawnee origin traditions, "the world was sung into being by a chorus of powerful voices." Tirawa-hat, the most powerful sky power, spoke to the other powers by means of Thunder and placed the sun, moon, and stars of the four directions in their proper places to provide structure to the universe. As the sky powers sang, water appeared, the earth emerged, plants and animals were created. Morning Star and Evening Star copulated, and a female child was born; then Sun and Moon copulated, and a male child was born. The children were transported to earth on a whirlwind, and from them all Pawnee human beings were born." Osages, who lived between the Missouri and Arkansas River when they first met Europeans, related stories of migration to that place and ultimately traced their origins to a meeting of heaven and earth. They divided themselves into two moieties and twenty-four patrilineal clans, each divided into several subclans. The nine clans of the Sky (Tsizhu) moiety came from the stars; with the help of Wah'-Kon-Tah, the guiding force of the universe, they found the fifteen clans of the Earth (Hon-ga) moiety and merged with them to become the Ni-U-Ko'n-Ska, the Children of the Middle Waters.

Navajos remember it differently. "Alk'idaa jiini" [Of a time long, long ago these things are said]: people emerged into this world from several lower worlds. "First Man stood on the eastern side of the First World. He represented the Dawn and was the Life Giver. First Woman stood opposite in the West. She represented Darkness and Death." First Man burned a crystal, and First Woman went to live with him. The beings in the First World were Mist People, with no definite form. In each world they fought, squabbled, and behaved badly, causing a breakdown of *hozoho* (harmony). Each time, they fled to a higher world, where they met new people. Antisocial behavior and conflict produced misfortune; proper relationships between the sexes, with other peoples, and with other living things were crucial to social harmony. Finally, they reached the present world. Dinetah, the Navajo homeland, took shape, bounded by four sacred mountains: Dook'o'ooslIfd (Abalone Shell Mountain, or San Francisco Peaks) to the west, Sis Naajini (Dawn or White Shell Mountain, Blanca Peak) to the east, Tsoodzil (Blue Bead or Turquoise Mountain, Mount Taylor) to the south, and Dibe Nitsaa (Obsidian Mountain, or Hesperus Peak) to the north. Changing Woman, also known as White Shell Woman, was found as a baby on top of Ch'ool'f'i (Gobernador Knob) and raised by First Man and First Woman. Changing Woman grew up, experienced her first Kinaalda (puberty ceremony), and raised twin sons, Monster Slayer and Child Born for Water. She went to live with her husband, the Sun, in the western ocean and created four clans who then returned to Dinetah, met the other Navajos living there, and found they spoke the same language. The People had moved from lower worlds of chaos and strife into a higher world of beauty and harmony and came together in a sacred place.

Among northern Plains peoples, origin stories often revolved around the actions of creator/trickster figures who often took animal form and other powers such as Sun and Wind, Moon and Stars. Creator figures differed, but stories often contained a common "earth diver" theme, in which animals or birds retrieved earth from below the surface of primal waters and the creator figures used it to bring the world into being. The people who told and heard the stories were culturally related to the creator figures and other characters, so the stories shaped identity as well as explained the world. Crow accounts, for example, portrayed the formation of the world before the Crows existed as a people but linked them with a uniquely Crow creator figure, Old Man Coyote. Together with his little coyote brother, Cirape, Old Man Coyote created the earth and placed plants, animals, and human beings on it. He taught human beings how to live, eat plants, make weapons, hunt animals, and cook food. Blackfeet told how Napi, or Old Man, whose father was the Sun and mother the Moon, "came from the south, making the mountains, the prairies, and the forests as he passed along . . . arranging the world as we see it today." He made the birds and animals and covered the plains with grass for the animals to feed on. Then he molded a woman and child out of clay, told them "You must be people," and taught them how to fend for themselves.

The idea that Indians came from Asia, filtering across Beringia like some ancient Ellis Island immigrants, angers many Native people, who dispute that "science can tell them where they came from." Lakota scholar Vine Deloria, Jr. dismisses the Beringian theory as a "white lie," something that "exists and existed only in the minds of scientists" and allows Euro-Americans to portray Indians as "latecomers who had barely unpacked before Columbus came knocking on the door." Disconnected in this scenario from their American roots, first Americans become relegated to the status of first immigrants.

Most scholars are more concerned with finding evidence than with perpetuating lies. Archaeological, dental, biological, and faunal evidence all suggest ancient links between Asia and America, though that is no guarantee that traffic was one way across Beringia or that this was the only migration route. If humans were here all along, they would, presumably, have left evidence of a presence that predated the retreat of the ice sheets. A reading of current archaeological literature suggests a drive to find this evidence rather than a conspiracy to defend a lie. But the strongest and most prolific evidence comes from the era when the Ice Age was in the last stages of retreat and Pleistocene mammals were becoming extinct.

In 1927, near Folsom, New Mexico, paleontologists from the Denver Museum of Natural History uncovered human artifacts near the bones of fossil bison believed to have been extinct for thousands of years, clear evidence that people had lived in the West since the late Pleistocene. Five years later, a road construction crew near Clovis, New Mexico, on the western edge of the Llano Estacado, or Staked Plain, unearthed a stone tool not far from a huge animal tooth. Archaeologists began excavations at the site, which became known as Blackwater Draw. They found distinctive fluted projectile points— "Clovis points"—mingled with mammoth bones. Other Clovis points were uncovered at sites throughout North America, providing the first well-documented culture and consistent evidence of human occupation in the West as much as 11,500 radiocarbon years (more than 13,000 calendar years) ago. Much of the evidence for an earlier human presence has been equivocal, and most scholars are reluctant to accept evidence that will not "stand up in court," but the assumption that the Clovis point people were the very first Americans is under increasing assault.

At Monte Verde in Chile, a group of people lived for a time on the banks of a stream as much as fifteen thousand years ago. In 1976 archaeologists excavated the wooden foundations of a dozen pole-frame houses, the oldest known village in the Americas. Among other evidence of human habitation they also found a child's footprint embedded in clay. Monte Verde is generally accepted as a pre-Clovis site. The new evidence from South America raised intriguing questions about North America and challenged the notion that Clovis points represented the work of the earliest inhabitants. If the first Americans came from Asia and pushed south as the ice sheets receded, how did these people happen to be in Chile so early? New climatic data and new radiocarbon calibrations for dating the Ice Age have now pushed back the whole timescale for first settlement.

Ancient America becomes a more complex place with each new discovery. In 1996 the skeleton of an adult male age between forty and fifty-five was discovered near the junction of the Snake and Columbia Rivers at Kennewick in Washington State. The skeleton showed evidence of violence, including a stone projectile point lodged in the left hip, and was estimated to be about 9,500 years old. But when physical archaeologists reported that the skeleton exhibited Caucasoid features, "Kennewick Man" became the center of a storm of controversy. Some people suggested the man was European rather than Native American; others argued he was too ancient to be clearly affiliated with any modern Indian group; the Nez Perce, Umatilla,

Wanapum, Yakima, and Colville tribes claimed him as their ancestor and demanded the return of the remains under the terms of the Native American Graves Protection and Repatriation Act of 1990. The Interior Department ordered the remains to be given to the tribes for reburial, but in August 2002, Justice John Jelderks, justice magistrate of the United States District Court in Portland, Oregon, found that scientists must be allowed access to the skeletal remains. The controversy and the questions continue.

Perhaps humans came long before the ice caps retreated. Perhaps they came by sea, plying skin boats along the Aleutian Islands across the Gulf of Alaska and then south along the deglaciated Pacific Coast before the first Clovis hunters and before the continental glaciers melted. They would have found numerous locations for habitation where coastal wildlife refuges offered easily exploitable resources of fish, birds, and sea mammals. Recent discoveries of two fishing and seabird-hunting campsites on the coast of Peru have been radiocarbon dated to as early as thirteen thousand years ago. Some scholars explain the remarkable diversity of Native languages—143 different languages—along the Pacific coast of North and Central America as the product of a process of successive splinterings from a common language that could have taken as long as thirty-five thousand years.

Low Bridge—Everybody Cross
Vine Deloria, Jr.

There are immense contemporary political implications to [the Bearing Strait migration] theory which make it difficult for many people to surrender. Considerable residual guilt remains over the manner in which the Western Hemisphere was invaded and settled by Europeans. Five centuries of brutality lie uneasily on the conscience, and consequently two beliefs have arisen which are used to explain away this dreadful history. People want to believe that the Western Hemisphere, and more particularly North America, was a vacant, unexploited, fertile land waiting to be put under cultivation according to God's holy dictates. As Woody Guthrie put it: "This Land is your land, this Land is my land." The hemisphere thus belonged to whoever was able to rescue it from its wilderness state.

Coupled with this belief is the idea that American Indians were not original inhabitants of the Western Hemisphere but latecomers who had barely unpacked before Columbus came knocking on the door. If Indians had arrived only a few centuries earlier, they had no *real* claim

From Vine Deloria, Jr., *Red Earth, White Lies* (New York: Scribner, 1995), 81-91, 106-7. Reprinted with permission.

to land that could not be swept away by European discovery. [In the first four decades of the twentieth century] Aleš Hrdlička of the Smithsonian devoted his life to the discrediting of any early occupancy of North America and a whole generation of scholars, fearfully following the master, rejected the claims of their peers rather than offend this powerful scholar. Finally, the embarrassing discovery that Clovis and Folsom points abounded in the western states forced the admission that the Indians might have beaten Columbus by quite a few centuries.

These ideas have great impact on how non-Indians view the claims for justice made by Indians. A personal experience may illuminate the impact of the Bering Strait on Indian rights. After Wounded Knee II in 1973, there were a number of trials of the people who had occupied the little village on the Pine Ridge Reservation in South Dakota. . . .

Several traditional people did not want evidence on the Bering Strait offered because they preferred to rely on their own view of how the Sioux people had come to be. Some wanted to talk about an origin from an underground world near Wind Cave, South Dakota; others thought that stories about living in or near the Gulf of Mexico would be sufficient; and still others wanted to discuss the stories about living in the far north, traditions which Werner Muller [an anthropologist who challenged the Bering Strait theory's time frame] had used in his new theory of the human occupancy of North America. None of these accounts would have been understood in a Nebraska courtroom no matter how sympathetic the judge, because they varied considerably with scientific beliefs about the Bering Strait. So some discussion was presented on the Bering Strait.

I was standing in the hallway of the courthouse smoking a Pall Mall (in those wonderful days when you and not your peers chose your vices) and a lady approached me all agiggle about what had taken place that morning. She gushed over what had been said about the Bering Strait as if she were the chairperson of an anthropology department and left me with the comment: "Well, dearie, we are all immigrants from somewhere." After reflecting on her comment for a moment, I wanted to run down the hallway after her and say, "Yes, indeed, but it makes one helluva difference whether we came 100,000 years ago or just out of boat steerage a generation back."

Her remark was symptomatic of the non-Indian response to the pleas of Indians. By making us immigrants to North America they are able to deny the fact that we were the full, complete, and total owners of this continent. They are able to see us simply as earlier interlopers and therefore throw back at us the accusation that we had simply *found* North America a little earlier than they had. On that basis, I would suppose, no nation actually *owns* the land its citizens live on, with the exception, if we accept early archaeological findings, of the people of Africa, where human evolution is believed to have begun. . . .

Most scholars today simply begin with the *assumption* that the Bering Strait migration doctrine was proved a long time ago and there is no need to plow familiar ground. Jesse D. Jennings and Edward Norbeck's *Prehistoric Man in the New World* provides a compendium of papers discussing the state of research and field investigations dealing with the earliest sites of human occupation in the Americas. The introductory article has a single sentence on the Bering Strait and the essays proceed without the slightest doubt that they are being built on a strong foundation. Since these scholars were so confident of the validity of the land bridge doctrine I assumed that there was, somewhere in scholarly publications, a detailed article which cited evidence and arguments that proved, beyond a reasonable doubt, that Paleo-Indians had at one time crossed from Asia into the Western Hemisphere. I was unable to find anything of this nature. . . .

Scholars and popular science writers, in discussing the Bering Strait doctrine, usually do not address the many real difficulties which this idea presents. They reach a point where they must sound intelligent to their peers and readers and promptly spin out a tale of stalwart hunters trekking across frozen tundra or frolicking in the suddenly warm Arctic meadows, and continue with their narrative. Looking at a map of the world, the proximity of Asia and Alaska seems too obvious to reject, but only rarely do scholars look at the map closely enough to see the absurdity of their claim. . . .

Presumably, the Paleo-Indians are living somewhere in eastern Siberia, having migrated there millennia ago. We will begin their journey with hunting bands living along the Kolyma River, at least half of which lies above the Artic Circle. Looking eastward they would find two formidable mountain ranges, the Khrebet Gydan and the Chukotskoye Nagor'ye, blocking their migration to the east. If and when they surmount these mountains and find their way to the shores of the eastern tip of Siberia, they must cross over the strait, and here most scholars insist that it was not a strait but a broad plain because the water that would have ordinarily covered it was locked up in the glacial sheet that covers North America in the eastern part of the continent. We will allow them to cross whatever the conditions.

Reaching the area we know as present-day Alaska, the people encounter a forbidding set of mountains both above and below the Arctic Circle. The Baird, Schawat, Endicott, and Shublik chains fence them on the north, the Kaiyuh and Kuskokwim Mountains are to the south, and on reaching the Canadian border they meet the Richardson Mountains and the continental divide of the northernmost chain of the Rocky Mountain group. To the south also are the Ogilvie Mountains and then the massive MacKenzie mountain chain with the smaller Franklin Mountains yet to the east. Finally, the hunters are out on a reasonably flat plain, although one that is not calculated to present a paradise for hunters, since it is, according to many scholars, covered in a thick glacial sheet. . . .

We have only traced the most likely route and given scholars the benefit of the doubt by locating the Paleo-Indians on the Kolyma River in eastern Siberia. Jared Diamond, discussing the big-game hunter migration which he believes took place around 12,000 years ago, says that "the colonists [of Siberia] probably came from eastern Europe, where Stone Age hunters in what is now the Ukraine built their houses out of neatly stacked bones of mammoths."

If we locate the migrating Paleo-Indians in the Ukraine, then it is necessary to add about a dozen more mountain ranges and a goodly number of high desertlike plateaus, a considerable stretch of tundra, and no one knows how many other obstacles. The point that must be understood is that nobody really knows; they just seem to make it up as they go along. To suggest a Ukrainian origin for people who migrated across the Bering Strait in turn suggests that they had something definite in mind in wandering eastward, and that supposition cannot be sustained at all. Almost every articulation of the Bering Strait theory is woefully deficient in providing a motive for the movement. . . .

It occurred to me that I might be able to find an essay devoted solely to the question of the validity of land bridges, written when a scholar had no thesis of migrating species to defend and when the Bering Strait migration did not come to mind. And indeed such an essay exists. George Gaylord Simpson was about as close to a living deity in evolutionary biology as Mother Nature herself, and one day he sat down and penned a little piece entitled "Mammals and Land Bridges." We can assume that what was applicable to mammals might be profitably applied to dinosaurs and perhaps even to Paleo people. Simpson uses a rather commonsense approach to the subject and suggests that only representatives of genera cross land bridges. A single genus does not by itself cross into new continents. More important, carnivores generally follow the herbivores they have been feasting on. "Where herbivores go, carnivores can and will accompany them, and carnivores cannot go where there are no herbivores. The postulation of land bridges on the basis of one or a few mammals is thus very uncertain. Unless there is a reasonable possibility that their companions have not been discovered, a theoretical bridge based on such evidence is probably unreal." In other words, if we do want to move horses and camels to Asia and bison to America, we will probably want to ensure that carnivores accompanied them if we wish to make our case.

The objection raised earlier regarding human, and then mammal and dinosaur, expeditions across the Bering Strait—that the route had to traverse a set of rugged mountain ranges on both sides of the Bering Strait—is regarded by Simpson as a major barrier even if a land bridge does exist. "For many of these animals, such as the monkeys, the absence of necessary environmental conditions beyond the bridge is an evident reason for their stopping where they did. Others, like the bison, were evidently kept by analogous environmental barriers from reaching the bridge." In other words, the bison simply would not have begun the tedious trip through the Siberian mountains, nor would horses and camels have tried to scale Scagway.

George Gaylord Simpson's conclusion, apparently unread or unheeded by several decades of scientific writers, is that "in the whole history of mammals there are exceedingly few cases (e.g., Lower Eocene between Europe and North America) where the evidence really warrants the inference of a wide-open corridor between two now distinct continental masses." This conclusion supports Werner Muller's Canada to Scandinavia-England-France thesis and does not give much comfort to the myriad of scholars who believe in the Bering Strait—for both animal and human migrations.

Not only does the more recent interpretation of human evolution militate against American Indians being latecomers to the Western Hemisphere, an examination of the Bering Strait doctrine suggests that such a journey would have been nearly impossible even if there had been hordes of Paleo-Indians trying to get across the hypothetical land bridge. It appears that not even animals or plants *really* crossed this mythical connection between Asia and North America. The Bering Strait exists and existed only in the minds of scientists.

Questions for Discussion

1. How should historians reckon with a debate between science and cultural traditions? Should historians accept different types of knowledge as equally valid, even when they seem contradictory? Or should they disregard myths that obscure actual historical events and try to uncover what "really happened"?

2. How does our perception of history change when we incorporate a long view of the past—attempting to uncover the stories of the very first people to inhabit the land we now call the United States—into the American narrative?

3. What is at stake for Indian people in this debate? For non- Indian people? Why does the origin of the Indians in North America matter?

4. Do American Indians have a special claim to the land rooted in their long history on it? Does their long occupancy of the continent give them a distinct identity from other Americans? What constitutes identity at its deepest source?

2

Colonial Society and Economy

Why Did Slavery Develop in the Colonies?

The first recorded African people arrived in the British mainland colonies in 1619, but historians do not know when black men and women were first enslaved by the colonists. The first slave codes referring to "negroes" did not appear in colonial statutes until the 1660s. What happened in the interim—the process by which slavery developed—has fascinated modern scholars. Did the system of African chattel slavery develop out of economic necessity, later drawing on race as a retrofitted justification for enslavement, or did black slavery grow out of existing racism among the colonists? Oscar and Mary Handlin built a case for the former scenario, maintaining that black slavery initially developed in response to the needs of colonial economy apart from racial prejudice. In the beginning, according to the Handlins, slaveholders focused on keeping their financial bottom line in the black without regard to the color of their servants. A decade after the Handlins published this provocative thesis, Carl Degler rebutted it by arguing that the colonists had arrived in the New World with racial prejudices that they quickly codified into a formal system of black slavery. From these origins, the dispute continues up to the present.

Slavery left a lasting stain on the American past and provides historians with an enduring enigma tangled in the roots of the American character. Scholars examine the Declaration of Independence with meticulous attention, word by word, trying to discern how Thomas Jefferson, its slaveholding author, could have listed among the self-evident truths "that all Men are created equal." Jefferson embodied the paradoxical American attitude toward slavery: He was uncomfortable with the institution—he even tried to interject into the Declaration a passage breathing moral outrage at the slave trade—yet remained a slaveowner to the end of his life.

How could the colonies, declaring a war for liberty, give so little notice to what today seems a glaring contradiction between their words and their deeds? And how could it be that the very idea of liberty, grounded in English tradition and nurtured in British North America, had grown up in the colonies side by side with its monstrous opposite? At some point—locating that point is the issue— British colonists in America transformed black servants into slaves. The authors of these opposing pieces ask how white perceptions of black Africans figured into that transformation. Did white racism present from the beginning provide the foundations of slavery, or did slavery come first, applied to Africans for circumstantial reasons that eventually bred racial prejudice? Whatever the answer, the authors do not perceive black slavery in North America as carefully and consciously planned. Its nineteenth-century character was not fully shaped in the seventeenth. Instead it developed. It developed because there was a system of servitude and inequality even for whites, because there was an African slave trade, and because there was racism among European colonists. These facts combined to produce an institution from which American society is still recovering; the order of their combination may determine how completely we are able to mend.

Origins of the Southern Labor System
Oscar and Mary F. Handlin

Through the first three-quarters of the seventeenth century, the Negroes, even in the South, were not numerous; nor were they particularly concentrated in any district. They came into a society in which a large part of the population was to some degree unfree; indeed in Virginia under the Company almost everyone, even tenants and la-

From Oscar and Mary F. Handlin, "Origins of the Southern Labor System," *William and Mary Quarterly* 7, no. 2 (April 1950): 199-222. Reprinted with permission.

borers, bore some sort of servile obligation. The Negroes' lack of freedom was not unusual. These newcomers, like so many others, were
accepted, bought and held, as kinds of servants. They were certainly
not well off. But their ill-fortune was of a sort they shared with men
from England, Scotland, and Ireland, and with the unlucky aborigenes
[*sic*] held in captivity. Like the others, some Negroes became free, that
is, terminated their period of service. Some became artisans; a few
became landowners and the masters of other men. The status of Negroes was that of servants; and so they were identified and treated
down to the 1660's.

The word, "slave" was, of course, used occasionally. It had no meaning in English law, but there was a significant colloquial usage. This
was a general term of derogation. . . .

It was in this sense that Negro servants were sometimes called
slaves. But the same appellation [*sic*] was, in England, given to other
non-English servants,—to a Russian, for instance. In Europe and in
the American colonies, the term was, at various times and places, applied indiscriminately to Indians, mulattoes, and mestizos, as well as
to Negroes. For that matter, it applied also to white Englishmen. It
thus commonly described the servitude of children; so, the poor
planters complained, "Our children, the parents dieinge" are held as
"slaues or drudges" for the discharge of their parents' debts. Penal
servitude too was often referred to as slavery; and the phrase, "slavish servant" turns up from time to time. Slavery had no meaning in
law; at most it was a popular description of a low form of service.

Yet in not much more than a half century after 1660 this term of
derogation was transformed into a fixed legal position. In a society
characterized by many degrees of unfreedom, the Negro fell into a
status novel to English law, into an unknown condition toward which
the colonists unsteadily moved, slavery in its eighteenth- and nineteenth-century form. The available accounts do not explain this development because they assume that this form of slavery was known
from the start.

Can it be said, for instance, that the seventeenth-century English-
man might have discovered elsewhere an established institution, the
archetype of slavery as it was ultimately defined, which seemed more
advantageous than the defined English customs for use in the New
World? The internationally recognized "slave trade" has been cited as
such an institution. But when one notes that the Company of Royal
Adventurers referred to their cargo as "Negers," "Negro-Servants,"
"Servants . . . from Africa," or "Negro Person," but rarely as slaves,
it is not so clear that it had in view some unique or different status.
And when one remembers that the transportation of Irish servants
was also known as the "slave-trade," then it is clear that those who

sold and those who bought the Negro, if they troubled to consider legal status at all, still thought of him simply as a low servant. . . .

Yet the Negroes did cease to be servants and became slaves, ceased to be men in whom masters held a proprietary interest and became chattels, objects that were the property of their owners. In that transformation originated the southern labor system.

Although the colonists assumed at the start that all servants would "fare alike in the colony," the social realities of their situation early gave rise to differences of treatment. It is not necessary to resort to racialist assumptions to account for such measures; these were simply the reactions of immigrants lost to the stability and security of home and isolated in an immense wilderness in which threats from the unknown were all about them. Like the millions who would follow, these immigrants longed in the strangeness for the company of familiar men and singled out to be welcomed those who were most like themselves. So the measures regulating settlement spoke specifically in this period of differential treatment for various groups. From time to time, regulations applied only to "those of our own nation," or to the French, the Dutch, the Italians, the Swiss, the Palatines, the Welsh, the Irish, or to combinations of the diverse nationalities drawn to these shores.

In the same way the colonists became aware of the differences between themselves and the African immigrants. The rudeness of the Negroes' manners, the strangeness of their languages, the difficulty of communicating to them English notions of morality and proper behavior occasioned sporadic laws to regulate their conduct. So, Bermuda's law to restrain the insolencies of Negroes "who are servents" (that is, their inclination to run off with the pigs of others) was the same in kind as the legislation that the Irish should "straggle not night or dai, as is too common with them." Until the 1660's the statutes on the Negroes were not at all unique. Nor did they add up to a decided trend.

But in the decade after 1660 far more significant differentiations with regard to term of service, relationship to Christianity, and disposal of children, cut the Negro apart from all other servants and gave a new depth to his bondage.

The question of length of service became critical when the mounting value of labor eased the fear that servants would be a drain on "vittles" and raised the expectation of profit from their toil. Those eager to multiply the number of available hands by stimulating immigration had not only to overcome the reluctance of a prospective newcomer faced with the trials of a sea journey; they had also to counteract the widespread reports in England and Scotland that servants were harshly treated and bound in perpetual slavery.

To encourage immigration therefore, the colonies embarked upon a line of legislation designed to improve servants' conditions and to enlarge the prospect of a meaningful release, a release that was not the start of a new period of servitude, but of life as a freeman and landowner. Thus Virginia, in 1642, discharged "publick tenants from their servitudes, who, like one sort of villians anciently in England" were attached to the lands of the governor; and later laws provided that no person was to "be adjudged to serve the collonie hereafter." Most significant were the statutes which reassured prospective newcomers by setting limits to the terms of servants without indentures, in 1638/9 in Maryland, in 1642/3 in Virginia. These acts seem to have applied only to voluntary immigrants "of our own nation." The Irish and other aliens, less desirable, at first received longer terms. But the realization that such discrimination retarded "the peopling of the country" led to an extension of the identical privilege to all Christians.

But the Negro never profited from these enactments. Farthest removed from the English, least desired, he communicated with no friends who might be deterred from following. Since his coming was involuntary, nothing that happened to him would increase or decrease his numbers. To raise the status of Europeans by shortening their terms would ultimately increase the available hands by inducing their compatriots to emigrate; to reduce the Negro's term would produce an immediate loss and no ultimate gain. By midcentury the servitude of Negroes seems generally lengthier than that of whites; and thereafter the consciousness dawns that the Blacks will toil for the whole of their lives, not through any particular concern with their status but simply by contrast with those whose years of labor are limited by statute. . . .

By the last quarter of the seventeenth century, one could distinguish clearly between the Negro slave who served for life and the servant for a period. But there was not yet a demarcation in personal terms: the servant was not yet a free man, nor the slave a chattel. As late as 1686, the words slave and servant could still be conflated to an extent that indicated men conceived of them as extensions of the same condition. A Frenchman in Virginia in that year noted, "There are degrees among the slaves brought here, for a Christian over 21 years of age cannot be held a slave more than five years, but the negroes and other infidels remain slaves all their lives."

It was the persistence of such conceptions that raised the fear that "noe free borne Christians will ever be induced to come over servants" without overwhelming assurance that there would be nothing slavish in their lot. After all Pennsylvania and New York now gave the European newcomer a choice of destination. In Virginia and Maryland there was a persistent effort to make immigration more attractive by further ameliorating the lot of European servants. . . .

Meanwhile the condition of the Negro deteriorated. In these very years, a startling growth in numbers complicated the problem. The Royal African Company was, to some extent, responsible, though its operations in the mainland colonies formed only a very minor part of its business. But the opening of Africa to free trade in 1698 inundated Virginia, Maryland, and South Carolina with new slaves. Under the pressure of policing these newcomers the regulation of Negroes actually grew harsher.

The early laws against runaways, against drunkenness, against carrying arms or trading without permission had applied penalties as heavy as death to all servants, Negroes and whites. But these regulations grew steadily less stringent in the case of white servants. On the other hand fear of the growing number of slaves, uneasy suspicion of plots and conspiracies, led to more stringent control of Negroes and a broad view of the master's power of discipline. Furthermore the emerging difference in treatment was calculated to create a real division of interest between Negroes on the one hand and whites on the other. Servants who ran away in the company of slaves, for instance, were doubly punished, for the loss of their own time and for the time of the slaves, a provision that discouraged such joint ventures. . . .

The first settlers in Virginia had been concerned with the difficulty of preserving the solidarity of the group under the disruptive effects of migration. They had been enjoined to "keepe to themselves" not to "marry nor give in marriage to the heathen, that are uncircumcised." But such resolutions were difficult to maintain and had gradually relaxed until the colonists included among "themselves" such groups as the Irish, once the objects of very general contempt. A common lot drew them together; and it was the absence of a common lot that drew these apart from the Negro. At the opening of the eighteenth century, the Black was not only set off by economic and legal status; he was "abominable," another order of man. . . .

Slavery had emerged in a society in which the unit of active agriculture was small and growing smaller; even the few large estates were operated by sub-division among tenants. After 1690, however, South Carolinians (and still later Georgians) turned from naval stores and the fur trade to the cultivation of rice, cotton, and indigo. In the production of these staples, which required substantial capital equipment, there was an advantage to large-scale operations. By then it was obvious which was the cheapest, most available, most exploitable labor supply. The immense profits from the tropical crops steadily sucked slaves in ever growing numbers into the plantation. With this extensive use, novel on the mainland, the price of slaves everywhere rose sharply, to the advantage of those who already held them. The prospect that the slaveowner would profit not only by the Negroes' labor, but also by the rise in their unit value and by their probable increase through breeding, accounted for the spread of the plantation to the older tobacco regions where large-scale production was not, as in the rice areas, necessarily an asset.

The new social and economic context impressed indelibly on the Negro the peculiar quality of chattel with which he had been left, as other servants escaped the general degradation that had originally been the common portion of all. Not only did the concentration of slaves in large numbers call for more rigid discipline, not only did the organization of the plantation with its separate quarters, hierarchy of overseers, and absentee owners widen the gulf between black and white, but the involvement of the whole southern economy in plantation production created an effective interest against any change in status. . . .

The distinctive qualities of the southern labor system were then not the simple products of the plantation. They were rather the complex outcome of a process by which the American environment broke down the traditional European conceptions of servitude. In that process the weight of the plantation had pinned down on the Negro the clearly-defined status of a chattel, a status left him as other elements in the population achieved their liberation.

Slavery and the Genesis of American Race Prejudice
Carl N. Degler

The Handlins' attempt to answer the question as to why slavery was slow in appearing in the statutes is, to me, not convincing. Essentially their explanation is that by the 1660's, for a number of reasons which do not have to be discussed here, the position of the white servant was improving, while that of the Negroes was sinking to slavery. In this manner, the Handlins contend, Negro and white servants, heretofore treated alike, attained different status. There are at least two major objections to this argument. First of all, their explanation, by depending upon the improving position of white servants as it does, cannot apply to New England, where servants were of minor importance. Yet the New England colonies, like the Southern, developed a

From Carl N. Degler, "Slavery and the Genesis of American Race Prejudice," *Comparative Studies in Society and History* 2, no. 1 (Oct. 1959), 49-66. Reprinted with permission.

system of slavery for the Negro that fixed him in a position of permanent inferiority. The greatest weakness of the Handlins' case is the difficulty in showing that the white servant's position was improving during and immediately after the 1660's.

Without attempting to go into any great detail on the matter, several acts of the Maryland and Virginia legislatures during the 1660's and 1670's can be cited to indicate that an improving status for white servants was at best doubtful. In 1662, Maryland restricted a servant's travel without a pass to two miles beyond his master's house; in 1671 the same colony lengthened the time of servants who arrived without indenture from four to five years. Virginia in 1668 provided that a runaway could be corporally punished and also have additional time exacted from him. If, as these instances suggest, the white servant's status was not improving, then we are left without an explanation for the differing status accorded white and Negro servants after 1660.

Actually, by asking why slavery developed late in the English colonies we are setting ourselves a problem which obscures rather than clarifies the primary question of why slavery in North America seemed to leave a different mark on the Negro than it did in South America. To ask why slavery in the English colonies produced discrimination against Negroes after 1660 is to make the tacit assumption that prior to the establishment of slavery there was none. If, instead, the question is put, "Which appeared first, slavery or discrimination?" then no prejudgment is made. Indeed, it now opens a possibility for answering the question as to why the slavery in the English colonies, unlike that in the Spanish and Portuguese, led to a caste position for Negroes, whether free or slave. In short, the recent work of the Handlins and the fact that slavery first appeared in the statutes of the English colonies forty years after the Negro's arrival, have tended to obscure the real possibility that the Negro was actually *never* treated as an equal of the white man, servant or free.

It is true that when Negroes were first imported into the English colonies there was no law of slavery and therefore whatever status they were to have would be the work of the future. This absence of a status for black men, which, it will be remembered was not true for the Spanish and Portuguese colonies, made it possible for almost any kind of status to be worked out. It was conceivable that they would be accorded the same status as white servants, as the Handlins have argued; it was also possible that they would not. It all depended upon the reactions of the people who received the Negroes.

It is the argument of this paper that the status of the Negro in the English colonies was worked out within a framework of discrimination; that from the outset, as far as the available evidence tells us, the Negro was treated as an inferior to the white man, servant or free. If this be true, then it would follow that as slavery evolved as a legal status, it reflected and included as a part of its essence, this same discrimination which white men had practised against the Negro all along and before any statutes decreed it. . . .

It is indeed true as the Handlins in their article have emphasized that before the seventeenth century the Negro was rarely called a slave. But this fact should not overshadow the historical evidence which points to the institution without employing the name. Because no discriminatory title is placed upon the Negro we must not think that he was being treated like a white servant; for there is too much evidence to the contrary. Although the growth of a fully developed slave law was slow, unsteady and often unarticulated in surviving records, this is what one would expect when an institution is first being worked out. It is not the same, however, as saying that no slavery or discrimination against the Negro existed in the first decades of the Negro's history in America.

As will appear from the evidence which follows, the kinds of discrimination visited upon Negroes varied immensely. In the early 1640's it sometimes stopped short of lifetime servitude or inheritable status—the two attributes of true slavery—in other instances it included both. But regardless of the form of discrimination, the important point is that from the 1630's up until slavery clearly appeared in the statutes in the 1660's, the Negroes were being set apart and discriminated against as compared with the treatment accorded Englishmen, whether servants or free. . . .

Negroes and slaves were singled out for special status in the years before 1650. A Virginia law of 1640 provided that "all masters" should try to furnish arms to themselves and "all those of their families which shall be capable of arms"—which would include servants—"(excepting negros)." Not until 1648 did Maryland get around to such a prohibition, when it was provided that no guns should be given to "any Pagan for killing meate or to any other use," upon pain of a heavy fine. At no time were white servants denied the right to bear arms; indeed, as these statutes inform us, they were enjoined to possess weapons.

One other class of discriminatory acts against Negroes in Virginia and Maryland before 1660 also deserves to be noticed. Three different times before 1660—in 1643, 1644 and 1658—the Virginia assembly (and in 1654, the Maryland legislature) included Negro and Indian women among the "tithables." But white servant women were never placed in such a category, inasmuch as they were not expected to work in the fields. From the beginning, it would seem, Negro women, whether free or bond, were treated by the law differently from white women servants.

It is not until the 1640's that evidence of a status for Negroes akin to slavery, and, therefore, something more than mere discrimination begins to appear in the sources. Two cases of punishment for runaway servants in 1640 throw some light on the working out of a differentiated status for Negroes. The first case concerned three runaways, of whom two were white men and the third a Negro. All three were given thirty lashes, with the white men having the terms owed their masters extended a year, at the completion of which they were to work for the colony for three more years. The other, "being a Negro named John Punch shall serve his said master or his assigns for the time of his natural Life here or elsewhere." Not only was the Negro's punishment the most severe, and for no apparent reason, but he was, in effect, reduced to slavery. It is also clear, however, that up until the issuing of the sentence, he must have had the status of a servant.

The second case, also of 1640, suggests that by that date some Negroes were already slaves. Six white men and a Negro were implicated in a plot to run away. The punishments meted out varied, but Christopher Miller "a dutchman" (a prime agent in the business) "was given the harshest treatment of all: thirty stripes, burning with an "R" on the cheek, a shackle placed on his leg for a year "and longer if said master shall see cause" and seven years of service for the colony upon completion of his time due his master. The only other one of the seven plotters to receive the stripes, the shackle and the "R" was the Negro Emanuel, but, significantly, he did not receive any sentence of work for the colony. Presumably he was already serving his master for a life-time—i.e., he was a slave. About this time in Maryland it does not seem to have been unusual to speak of Negroes as slaves, for in 1642 one "John Skinner mariner" agreed "to deliver unto . . . Leonard Calvert, fourteen negro-men-slaves and three women-slaves." . . .

Concurrently with these examples of onerous service or actual slavery of Negroes, there were of course other members of the race who did gain their freedom. But the presence of Negroes rising out of servitude to freedom does not destroy the evidence that others were sinking into slavery; it merely underscores the unsteady evolution of a slave status. The supposition that the practice of slavery long antedated the law is strengthened by the tangential manner in which recognition of Negro slavery first appeared in the Virginia statutes. It occurred in 1660 in a law dealing with punishments for runaway servants, where casual reference was made to those "negroes who are incapable of making satisfaction by addition of time," since they were already serving for life.

Soon thereafter, as various legal questions regarding the status of Negroes came to the fore, the institution was further defined by statute law. In 1662 Virginia provided that the status of the offspring of a white man and a Negro would follow that of the mother—an interesting and unexplained departure from the common law and a reversion to Roman law. The same law stated that "any christian" fornicating "with a negro man or woman . . . shall pay double the fines imposed by the former act.". . .

As early as 1669 the Virginia law virtually washed its hands of protecting the Negro held as a slave. It allowed punishment of refractory slaves up to and including accidental death, relieving the master, explicitly, of any fear of prosecution, on the assumption that no man would "destroy his owne estate."

In fact by 1680 the law of Virginia had erected a high wall around the Negro. One discerns in the phrase "any negro or other slave" how the word "negro" had taken on the meaning of slave. Moreover, in the act of 1680 one begins to see the lineaments of the later slave codes. No Negro may carry any weapon of any kind, nor leave his master's grounds without a pass, nor shall "any negroe or other slave . . . presume to lift his hand in opposition against any Christian," and if a Negro runs away and resists recapture it "shalbe lawful for such person or persons to kill said negroe or slave. . . ."

Yet it would be a quarter of a century before Negroes would comprise even a fifth of the population of Virginia. Thus long before slavery or black labor became an important part of the Southern economy, a special and inferior status had been worked out for the Negroes who came to the English colonies. Unquestionably it was a demand for labor which dragged the Negro to American shores, but the status which he acquired here cannot be explained by reference to that economic motive. Long before black labor was as economically important as unfree white labor, the Negro had been consigned to a special discriminatory status which mirrored the social discrimination Englishmen practised against him. . . .

It would seem, then, that instead of slavery being the root of the discrimination visited upon the Negro in America, slavery was itself molded by the early colonists' discrimination against the outlander. In the absence of any law of slavery or commandments of the Church to the contrary—as was true of Brazil and Spanish-America—the institution of slavery into which the African was placed in the English colonies inevitably mirrored that discrimination and, in so doing, perpetuated it.

Once the English embodied their discrimination against the Negro in slave law, the logic of the law took over. Through the early eighteenth century, judges and legislatures in all the colonies elaborated the law along the discriminatory lines laid down in the amorphous beginnings. In doing so, of course, especially in the South, they had the added incentive of perpetuating and securing a labor system which by then had become indispensable to the economy. The cleavage between the races was in that manner deepened and hardened into the shape which became quite familiar by the nineteenth century. In due time, particularly in the South, the correspondence between the black man and slavery would appear so perfect that it would be difficult to believe that the Negro was fitted for anything other than the degraded status in which he was almost always found. It would also be forgotten that the discrimination had begun long before slavery had come upon the scene.

Questions for Discussion

1. Did the system of African chattel slavery develop out of economic necessity, or was it simply an outgrowth of racism already ingrained in the British colonists? Are the two mutually exclusive?

2. Why did the colonists eventually turn to using African slaves? Why didn't they continue using indentured servants from England or enslave the American Indians instead?

3. Was there an alternative to the African slave system? How might the colonial experience have been different without slavery? How might our nation's history look different?

4. Note the timing of these articles: The most contentious arguments about colonial slavery arose during the twentieth-century Civil Rights Movement. Why might the origins of slavery seem so important to historians at that time?

3

A More Perfect Union

How Democratic Is the United States Constitution?

On the second floor of Jacob Graff's brick house at the corner of Market and Seventh Street, on the outskirts of Philadelphia in June 1776, Thomas Jefferson sat writing:

> We hold these truths to be self-evident, that all men are created equal, that they are endowed by their Creator with certain unalienable Rights, that among these are Life, Liberty, and the pursuit of Happiness—That, to secure these rights, Governments are instituted among Men, deriving their just powers from the consent of the governed. . . .

The Declaration of Independence announced the sovereignty of the "thirteen united States of America," but they said very little about what independence actually looked like. That job was left to the men who ratified the Constitution—men like James Madison, who (along with Alexander Hamilton and John Jay) argued for ratification in a series of essays known today as *The Federalist*, as well as men like Patrick Henry, who passionately urged his fellow Virginians to reject the proposed Constitution. Theirs was the task of translating the ideals of the American Revolution into a system of government that would sustain the new nation.

From the heady days of 1776, it took eleven more years before the Constitution we know today was submitted to the American people, and nearly another year before its ratification was secured. During that time, the ideas that form the foundation of the American system of government were threshed out in the state constitutions, the Articles of Confederation, and ultimately the hard-fought debates over the creation and ratification of the federal Constitution. The leaders of the newly-independent nation wrestled with questions of how to translate Revolutionary ideals into a viable system of government, how democratic that system should be, and how it might reconcile the tension between traditional republican virtues and developing notions of liberalism.

The meaning of what these framers wrought during that summer of 1787 in Philadelphia is one of the great pursuits in the study of American history (not to mention jurisprudence), but if anything is clear after more than two centuries of scholarship and interpretation, it is that the meaning cannot be apprehended simply from the words on parchment. The significance of the Constitution must be sought in the process that created it, a process that was not confined to a few months in Philadelphia but had begun long before and crystallized during the debate over ratification, a process plotted along the points of compromises, shaped by the forces of ideological commitment, and tempered by the experience and interest of the men and women who gave form to the American system of government.

During the ratification debates running from 1787 to 1789, partisans generally coalesced into two opposed camps. Those who supported the Constitution seized the term Federalists, although they might have more correctly been called nationalists for their advocacy of a strong central government to encourage stability and trade. Those who opposed the proposed Constitution were stuck with the negative label of Antifederalists. They feared that an expanded national government was dangerous to the liberties of the states, which were themselves the guardians of individual freedom. Madison responded for the Federalists that only large republics were diverse enough to sufficiently diffuse the tyranny of a bare majority infringing on the rights of a minority. However, to ease the fears of Antifederalists and persuade them to adopt the Constitution, the Federalists promised to amend it with a Bill of Rights guaranteeing the liberties of the people. Even so, Antifederalists like Patrick Henry were wary of the power vested in the new government and uneasy about the direction that the grand American experiment—one that he, Madison, and other patriots had fought so hard to realize—was taking.

The Federalist Number 10
James Madison

November 22, 1787

Among the numerous advantages promised by a well constructed Union, none deserves to be more accurately developed than its tendency to break and control the violence of faction. . . .

By a faction, I understand a number of citizens, whether amounting to a majority or a minority of the whole, who are united and actuated by some common impulse of passion, or of interest, adverse to the rights of other citizens, or to the permanent and aggregate interests of the community.

There are two methods of curing the mischiefs of faction: the one, by removing its causes; the other, by controlling its effects.

There are again two methods of removing the causes of faction: the one, by destroying the liberty which is essential to its existence; the other, by giving to every citizen the same opinions, the same passions, and the same interests.

It could never be more truly said than of the first remedy, that it was worse than the disease. Liberty is to faction what air is to fire, an aliment without which it instantly expires. But it could not be less folly to abolish liberty, which is essential to political life, because it nourishes faction, than it would be to wish the annihilation of air, which is essential to animal life, because it imparts to fire its destructive agency.

The second expedient is as impracticable as the first would be unwise. As long as the reason of man continues fallible, and he is at liberty to exercise it, different opinions will be formed. . . . and from the influence of these on the sentiments and views of the respective proprietors, ensues a division of the society into different interests and parties.

The latent causes of faction are thus sown in the nature of man; and we see them everywhere. . . . A zeal for different opinions concerning religion, concerning government, and many other points, as well of speculation as of practice; an attachment to different leaders ambitiously contending for pre-eminence and power; or to persons of other descriptions whose fortunes have been interesting to the human passions, have, in turn, divided mankind into parties, inflamed them with mutual animosity, and rendered them much more disposed to vex

From James Madison, "X [Number 10]," in [Alexander Hamilton, James Madison, and John Jay], *The Federalist: A Collection of Essays, Written in Favour of the New Constitution, as Agreed Upon by the Federal Convention, September 17, 1787*, vol. 1 (New York: J. and A. M'Lean, 1788), 52-61.

and oppress each other than to co-operate for their common good. So strong is this propensity of mankind to fall into mutual animosities, that where no substantial occasion presents itself, the most frivolous and fanciful distinctions have been sufficient to kindle their unfriendly passions and excite their most violent conflicts. But the most common and durable source of factions has been the various and unequal distribution of property. Those who hold and those who are without property have ever formed distinct interests in society. Those who are creditors, and those who are debtors, fall under a like discrimination. A landed interest, a manufacturing interest, a mercantile interest, a moneyed interest, with many lesser interests, grow up of necessity in civilized nations, and divide them into different classes, actuated by different sentiments and views. The regulation of these various and interfering interests forms the principal task of modern legislation, and involves the spirit of party and faction in the necessary and ordinary operations of the government.

No man is allowed to be a judge in his own cause, because his interest would certainly bias his judgment, and, not improbably, corrupt his integrity. With equal, nay with greater reason, a body of men are unfit to be both judges and parties at the same time; yet what are many of the most important acts of legislation, but so many judicial determinations, not indeed concerning the rights of single persons, but concerning the rights of large bodies of citizens? And what are the different classes of legislators but advocates and parties to the causes which they determine? . . . The apportionment of taxes on the various descriptions of property is an act which seems to require the most exact impartiality; yet there is, perhaps, no legislative act in which greater opportunity and temptation are given to a predominant party to trample on the rules of justice. Every shilling with which they overburden the inferior number, is a shilling saved to their own pockets.

It is in vain to say that enlightened statesmen will be able to adjust these clashing interests, and render them all subservient to the public good. Enlightened statesmen will not always be at the helm. Nor, in many cases, can such an adjustment be made at all without taking into view indirect and remote considerations, which will rarely prevail over the immediate interest which one party may find in disregarding the rights of another or the good of the whole.

The inference to which we are brought is, that the *causes* of faction cannot be removed, and that relief is only to be sought in the means of controlling its *effects*.

If a faction consists of less than a majority, relief is supplied by the republican principle, which enables the majority to defeat its sinister views by regular vote. It may clog the administration, it may convulse the society; but it will be unable to execute and mask its violence under the forms of the Constitution. When a majority is included in a faction, the form of popular government, on the other hand, enables it to sacrifice to its ruling passion or interest both the public good and the rights of other citizens. To secure the public good and private rights against the danger of such a faction, and at the same time to preserve the spirit and the form of popular government, is then the great object to which our inquiries are directed. . . .

By what means is this object attainable? Evidently by one of two only. Either the existence of the same passion or interest in a majority at the same time must be prevented, or the majority, having such coexistent passion or interest, must be rendered, by their number and local situation, unable to concert and carry into effect schemes of oppression. If the impulse and the opportunity be suffered to coincide, we well know that neither moral nor religious motives can be relied on as an adequate control. . . .

From this view of the subject it may be concluded that a pure democracy, by which I mean a society consisting of a small number of citizens, who assemble and administer the government in person, can admit of no cure for the mischiefs of faction. A common passion or interest will, in almost every case, be felt by a majority of the whole; a communication and concert result from the form of government itself; and there is nothing to check the inducements to sacrifice the weaker party or an obnoxious individual. Hence it is that such democracies have ever been spectacles of turbulence and contention; have ever been found incompatible with personal security or the rights of property; and have in general been as short in their lives as they have been violent in their deaths. Theoretic politicians, who have patronized this species of government, have erroneously supposed that by reducing mankind to a perfect equality in their political rights, they would, at the same time, be perfectly equalized and assimilated in their possessions, their opinions, and their passions.

A republic, by which I mean a government in which the scheme of representation takes place, opens a different prospect, and promises the cure for which we are seeking. . . . The two great points of difference between a democracy and a republic are: first, the delegation of the government, in the latter, to a small number of citizens elected by the rest; secondly, the greater number of citizens, and greater sphere of country, over which the latter may be extended.

The effect of the first difference is, on the one hand, to refine and enlarge the public views, by passing them through the medium of a chosen body of citizens, whose wisdom may best discern the true interest of their country, and whose patriotism and love of justice will be least likely to sacrifice it to temporary or partial considerations. Under such a regulation, it may well happen that the public voice, pronounced by the representatives of the people, will be more consonant to the public good than if pronounced by the people them-selves, convened for the purpose. On the other hand, the effect may be inverted. Men of factious tempers, of local prejudices, or of sinis-ter designs, may, by intrigue, by corruption, or by other means, first obtain the suffrages, and then betray the interests, of the people. The question resulting is, whether small or extensive republics are more favorable to the election of proper guardians of the public weal; and it is clearly decided in favor of the latter by two obvious considera-tions:

In the first place, it is to be remarked that, however small the re-public may be, the representatives must be raised to a certain num-ber, in order to guard against the cabals of a few; and that, however large it may be, they must be limited to a certain number, in order to guard against the confusion of a multitude. . . .

In the next place, as each representative will be chosen by a greater number of citizens in the large than in the small republic, it will be more difficult for unworthy candidates to practice with success the vicious arts by which elections are too often carried; and the suffrages of the people being more free, will be more likely to centre in men who possess the most attractive merit and the most diffusive and es-tablished characters.

It must be confessed that in this, as in most other cases, there is a mean, on both sides of which inconveniences will be found to lie. By enlarging too much the number of electors, you render the rep-resentatives too little acquainted with all their local circumstances and lesser interests; as by reducing it too much, you render him unduly attached to these, and too little fit to comprehend and pursue great and national objects. The federal Constitution forms a happy combi-nation in this respect; the great and aggregate interests being referred to the national, the local and particular to the State legislatures.

The other point of difference is, the greater number of citizens and extent of territory which may be brought within the compass of re-publican than of democratic government; and it is this circumstance principally which renders factious combinations less to be dreaded in the former than in the latter. The smaller the society, the fewer prob-ably will be the distinct parties and interests composing it; the fewer the distinct parties and interests, the more frequently will a majority be found of the same party; and the smaller the number of individ-uals composing a majority, and the smaller the compass within which they are placed, the more easily will they concert and execute their plans of oppression. Extend the sphere, and you take in a greater va-riety of parties and interests; you make it less probable that a ma-jority of the whole will have a common motive to invade the rights of other citizens; or if such a common motive exists, it will be more difficult for all who feel it to discover their own strength, and to act in unison with each other. Besides other impediments, it may be remarked that, where there is a consciousness of unjust or dishonorable purposes, communication is always checked by distrust in proportion to the number whose concurrence is necessary.

Hence, it clearly appears, that the same advantage which a republic has over a democracy, in controlling the effects of faction, is enjoyed by a large over a small republic,—is enjoyed by the Union over the States composing it. . . .

The influence of factious leaders may kindle a flame within their particular States, but will be unable to spread a general conflagration through the other States. A religious sect may degenerate into a political faction in a part of the Confederacy; but the variety of sects dispersed over the entire face of it must secure the national councils against any danger from that source. A rage for paper money, for an abolition of debts, for an equal division of property, or for any other improper or wicked project, will be less apt to pervade the whole body of the Union than a particular member of it; in the same proportion as such a malady is more likely to taint a particular county or district, than an entire State.

In the extent and proper structure of the Union, therefore, we behold a republican remedy for the diseases most incident to republican government. And according to the degree of pleasure and pride we feel in being republicans, ought to be our zeal in cherishing the spirit and supporting the character of Federalists.

Speech Before the Virginia State Ratifying Convention*
Patrick Henry
June 5, 1788

I am not free from suspicion: I am apt to entertain doubts: I rose yesterday to ask a question, which arose in my own mind. When I asked that question, I thought the meaning of my interrogation was

---

*The debate over the Constitution took place in an era before the modern standardization of spelling or punctuation. I have generally left spelling and grammar uncorrected except in a few instances of potentially confusing misspellings, but I have inserted paragraph breaks where it seemed appropriate to make the speech more accessible to the reader.

From Patrick Henry, "[Speech Before the Virginia State Ratifying Convention, June 5, 1788]," in *Debates and Other Proceedings of the Convention of Virginia, Convened at Richmond, on Monday the 2d day of June, 1788, for the Purpose of Deliberating on the Constitution Recommended by the Grand Federal Convention* (Petersburg, VA: Hunter and Prentis, 1788), 56-75.

obvious: The fate of this question and America may depend on this: Have they said, we the States? Have they made a proposal of a compact between States? If they had, this would be a confederation: It is otherwise most clearly a consolidated government. The question turns, Sir, on that poor little thing—the expression, *We, the people*, instead of the States of America. I need not take much pains to shew, that the principles of this system, are extremely pernicious, impolitic, and dangerous. . . .

Here is a revolution as radical as that which separated us from Great Britain. It is as radical, if in this transition our rights and privileges are endangered, and the sovereignty of the States be relinquished: And cannot we plainly see, that this is actually the case? The rights of conscience, trial by jury, liberty of the press, all your immunities and franchises, all pretensions to human rights and privileges, are rendered insecure, if not lost, by this change so loudly talked of by some, and inconsiderately by others. Is this same relinquishment of rights worthy of freemen? Is it worthy of that manly fortitude that ought to characterize republicans: It is said eight States have adopted this plan. I declare that if twelve States and an half had adopted it, I would with manly firmness, and in spite of an erring world, reject it. You are not to inquire how your trade may be increased, nor how you are to become a great and powerful people, but how your liberties can be secured; for liberty ought to be the direct end of your Government. . . .

We are come hither to preserve the poor Commonwealth of Virginia, if it can be possibly done: Something must be done to preserve your liberty and mine: The Confederation; this same despised Government, merits, in my opinion, the highest encomium: It carried us through a long and dangerous war: It rendered us victorious in that bloody conflict with a powerful nation: It has secured us a territory greater than any European Monarch possesses: And shall a Government which has been thus strong and vigorous, be accused of imbecility and abandoned for want of energy? Consider what you are about to do before you part with this Government. Take longer time in reckoning things: Revolutions like this have happened in almost every country in Europe: Similar examples are to be found in ancient Greece and ancient Rome: Instances of the people loosing their liberty by their own carelessness and the ambition of a few.

We are cautioned by the Honorable Gentleman who presides, against faction and turbulence: I acknowledge that licentiousness is dangerous, and that it ought to be provided against: I acknowledge also the new form of Government may effectually prevent it: Yet, there is another thing it will as effectually do: it will oppress and ruin the people. There are sufficient guards placed against sedition and licentiousness: For when power is given to this Government to suppress these, or, for any other purpose, the language it assumes is clear, express, and unequivocal, but when this Constitution speaks of privileges, there is an ambiguity, Sir, a fatal ambiguity. . . .

I mean, when it says, that there shall not be more Representatives, than one for every 30,000. Now, Sir, how easy is it to evade this privilege? "The number shall not exceed one for every 30,000." This may be satisfied by one Representative from each State. Let our numbers be ever so great, this immence continent, may, by this artful expression, be reduced to have but 13 Representatives: I confess this construction is not natural; but the ambiguity of the expression lays a good ground for a quarrel. Why was it not clearly and unequivocally expressed, that they *should* be entitled, to have one for every 30,000? . . .

I shall be told I am continually afraid: But, Sir, I have strong cause of apprehension: In some parts of the plan before you, the great rights of freemen are endangered, in other parts absolutely taken away. . . . But we are told that we need not fear, because those in power being our Representatives, will not abuse the powers we put in their hands: I am not well versed in history, but I will submit to your recollection, whether liberty has been destroyed most often by the licentiousness of the people, or by the tyranny of rulers? I imagine, Sir, you will find the balance on the side of tyranny. . . .

My great objection to this Government is, that it does not leave us the means of defending our rights; or, of waging war against tyrants: It is urged by some Gentlemen, that this new plan will bring us an acquisition of strength, an army, and the militia of the States: This is an idea extremely ridiculous: Gentlemen cannot be in earnest. This acquisition will trample on your fallen liberty: Let my beloved Americans guard against that fatal lethargy that has pervaded the universe: Have we the means of resisting disciplined armies, when our only defence, the militia is put into the hands of Congress?

The Honorable Gentleman said, that great danger would ensue if the Convention rose without adopting this system: I ask, where is that danger? I see none. . . . If, Sir, there was any, I would recur to the American spirit to defend us;—that spirit which has enabled us to surmount the greatest difficulties: To that illustrious spirit I address my most fervent prayer, to prevent our adopting a system destructive to liberty. . . .

To encourage us to adopt it, they tell us, that there is a plain easy way of getting amendments: When I come to contemplate this part, I suppose that I am mad, or, that my countrymen are so: The way to amendment, is, in my conception, shut. Let us consider this plain easy way: "The Congress, whenever two-thirds of both Houses shall deem it necessary, shall propose amendments to this Constitution, or, on the application of the Legislatures of two-thirds of the several States, shall call a Convention for proposing amendments, which, in either case, shall be valid to all intents and purposes, as part of this Constitution, when ratified by the Legislatures of three-fourths of the several States, or by Conventions in three-fourths thereof, as the one or the other mode of ratification may be proposed by the Congress." . . .

Let us consider the consequences of this: However uncharitable it may appear, yet I must tell my opinion, that the most unworthy characters may get into power and prevent the introduction of amendments: Let us suppose (for the case is supposeable, possible, and probable) that you happen to deal these powers to unworthy hands; will they relinquish powers already in their possession, or, agree to amendments? Two-thirds of the Congress, or, of the State Legislatures, are necessary even to propose amendments: If one-third of these be unworthy men, they may prevent the application for amendments; but what is destructive and mischievous is, that three-fourths of the State Legislatures, or of State Conventions, must concur in the amendments when proposed: In such numerous bodies, there must necessarily be some designing bad men: To suppose that so large a number as three-fourths of the States will concur, is to suppose that they will possess genius, intelligence, and integrity, approaching to miraculous. . . .

It is, Sir, a most fearful situation, when the most contemptible minority can prevent the alteration of the most oppressive Government; for it may in many respects prove to be such: Is this the spirit of republicanism? What, Sir, is the genius of democracy? . . . This, Sir, is the language of democracy; that a majority of the community have a right to alter their Government when found to be oppressive: But how different is the genius of your new Constitution from this? How different from the sentiments of freemen, that a contemptible minority can prevent the good of the majority? If then Gentlemen standing on this ground, are come to that point, that they are willing to bind themselves and their posterity to be oppressed, I am amazed and inexpressibly astonished. . . .

Our situation will be deplorable indeed: Nor can we ever expect to get this government amended, since I have already shewn, that a very small minority may prevent it; and that small minority interested in the continuance of the oppression: Will the oppressor let go the oppressed? Was there ever an instance? Can the annals of mankind exhibit one single example, where rulers overcharged with power, willingly let go the oppressed, though solicited and requested most earnestly? The application for amendments will therefore be fruitless. Sometimes the oppressed have got loose by one of those bloody struggles that desolate a country. A willing relinquishment of power is one of those things which human nature never was, nor ever will be capable of: The Honorable Gentleman's observations respecting the people's right of being the agents in the formation of this Government, are not accurate in my humble conception. The distinction between a National Government and a Confederacy is not sufficiently discerned.

Had the delegates who were sent to Philadelphia a power to propose a Consolidated Government instead of a Confederacy? . . . the American spirit, assisted by the ropes and chains of consolidation, is about to convert this country to a powerful and mighty empire: If you make the citizens of this country agree to become the subjects of one great consolidated empire of America, your Government will not have sufficent energy to keep them together: Such a Government is incompatible with the genius of republicanism: There will be no checks, no real balances, in this Government: What can avail your specious imaginary balances, your rope-dancing, chain-rattling, ridiculous ideal checks and contrivances? . . .

Consider our situation, Sir: Go to the poor man, ask him what he does; he will inform you, that he enjoys the fruits of his labour, under his own fig-tree, with his wife and children around him, in peace and security. Go to every other member of the society, you will find the same tranquil ease and content; you will find no alarms or disturbances: Why then tell us of dangers to terrify us into an adoption of this new Government? and yet who knows the dangers that this new system may produce; they are out of the sight of the common people: They cannot foresee latent consequences: I dread the operation of it on the middling and lower class of people: It is for them I fear the adoption of this system. I fear I tire the patience of the Committee, but I beg to be indulged with a few more observations. . . . I see great jeopardy in this new Government. I see none from our present one: I hope some Gentleman or other will bring forth, in full array, those dangers, if there be any, that we may see and touch them. . . .

Besides the expences of maintaining the Senate and other House in as much splendor as they please, there is to be a great and mighty President, with very extensive powers; the powers of a King: He is to be supported in extravagant magnificence: So that the whole of our property may be taken by this American Government, by laying what taxes they please, giving themselves what salaries they please, and suspending our laws at their pleasure. . . .

This Constitution is said to have beautiful features; but when I come to examine these features, Sir, they appear to me horridly frightful: Among other deformities, it has an awful squinting; it squints towards monarchy: And does not this raise indignation in the breast of every American? Your President may easily become King: Your Senate is so imperfectly constructed that your dearest rights may be sacrificed by what may be a small minority; and a very small minority may continue forever unchangeably this Government, although horridly defective: Where are your checks in this Government? . . . I would rather infinitely, and I am sure most of this Convention are of the same opinion, have a King, Lords, and Commons, than a Government so replete with such insupportable evils. . . .

The honorable member has said that we shall be properly represented: Remember, Sir, that the number of our Representatives is but ten, whereof six is a majority. Will these men be possessed of sufficient information? A particular knowledge of particular districts will not suffice. They must be well acquainted with agriculture, commerce, and a great variety of other matters throughout the Continent: They must know not only the actual state of nations in Europe, and America, the situation of their farmers, cottagers, and mechanics, but also the relative situation and intercourse of those nations. Virginia is as large as England. Our proportion of Representatives is but ten men. In England they have 530. The House of Commons in England, numerous as they are, we are told, is bribed, and have bartered away the rights of their constituents: What then shall become of us? Will these few protect our rights? Will they be incorruptible? You say they will be better men than the English Commoners. I say they will be infinitely worse men, because they are to be chosen blindfolded: Their election (the term, as applied to their appointment, is inaccurate) will be an involuntary nomination, and not a choice.

I have, I fear, fatigued the Committee, yet I have not said the one hundred thousandth part of what I have on my mind, and wish to impart. . . . I did not come prepared to speak on so multifarious a subject, in so general a manner. I trust you will indulge me another time.—Before you abandon the present system, I hope you will consider not only its defects, most maturely, but likewise those of that which you are to substitute to it. May you be fully apprised of the dangers of the latter, not by fatal experience, but by some abler advocate than me.

Questions for Discussion

1. Why did the Federalists claim that the nation needed a new form of government? What were their primary concerns about the United States under the Articles of Confederation? What were the Antifederalists' principal objections to the Constitution?

2. Why does Madison portray democracy as a threat to liberty? How are Patrick Henry's views different? Why did Henry fear for the welfare of the lower and "middling" classes under the Constitution?

3. Has the American political system validated Madison's predictions? Have any of Patrick Henry's fears been realized?

4. How do the Federalist and Antifederalist assessments of the Constitution contribute to our understanding of it today? As we get farther away from that summer in Philadelphia, what, if anything, can we infer about the "original intent" of the framers, and how should we apply it to questions and issues today that they could not have foreseen?

4

The Second Great Awakening

Mysterious Ways: What Moved Americans to Religious Revival?

In the autumn of 1821 in upstate New York, a twenty-nine-year-old lawyer in training named Charles Grandison Finney had a profound life-changing experience. As he recounted it in his *Memoirs*:

> the Holy Spirit descended upon me in a manner that seemed to go through me, body and soul. I could feel the impression, like a wave of electricity, going through and through me. Indeed it seemed to come in waves and waves of liquid love; for I could not express it in any other way. It seemed like the very breath of God. I can recollect distinctly that it seemed to fan me, like immense wings.

Although his testimony stands out for its eloquence, Finney's experience was hardly anomalous: During the first half of the nineteenth century a spiritual awakening swept across the United States. From the edges of the western frontier to the urban centers of the East, Protestant revival meetings inspired Americans in droves to convert or rededicate their lives to the Christian faith and the social reforms it demanded. Historians Paul E. Johnson and Nathan O. Hatch generally agree that the pervasive revival spirit of this Second Great Awakening (dubbed a sequel to a period of similarly intense religious ferment in the years before the Revolution) played a crucial role in the transformation of American society during the Jacksonian era, but they are divided over what that role was.

Paul Johnson centers his study on Charles Finney, who after his dramatic conversion went on to become one of the greatest revival preachers of the period. Johnson examines Finney's most celebrated revival, staged in 1830 and 1831 in the city of Rochester in western New York State. At the time, Rochester was a booming industrial center on the recently-completed Erie Canal at the heart of a region so inflamed with revivalism that it came to be called the "burned-over district." So successfully did Finney win over the city's businessmen, artisans, and workers with his rapturous preaching that Johnson has christened the revival a "shopkeeper's millennium." He concludes that revivalism in Rochester and beyond amounted to a form of class-based social control, a way for middle-class businessmen to impose their values on their workers. Nathan Hatch, to the contrary, surveys American religion over the entire period between the Revolution and the Civil War and determines that, instead of acting as a mechanism of social control, Christian revivalism made society more democratic.

A Shopkeeper's Millennium
Paul E. Johnson

Alexis de Tocqueville came [from France to travel throughout] the United States in the spring of 1831. He noted the first day that Americans were a profoundly religious people, and during his travels he asked scores of ministers and laymen why that was so. He always received the same reply: religion was strong in America because it was necessary, and it was necessary because Americans were free. A society with fixed ranks and privileges controls its members and has no need for religion. But a free society must teach men to govern themselves, and there is no greater inducement to self-restraint than belief in God. "Despotism," Tocqueville concluded, "may govern without faith, but liberty cannot."

Tocqueville was among the first to link revival religion with the concept of social control. Many have followed, and most of these share his central insight and repeat his central mistakes. The insight is enduring and valuable: in a society that lacked external controls, revivals

From Paul E. Johnson, *A Shopkeeper's Millennium: Society and Revivals in Rochester, New York, 1815-1837* (New York: Hill and Wang, 1978), 136-41. Reprinted with permission.

created order through individual self-restraint. But Tocqueville refused to ground either religion or the social discipline that derived from it in specific social processes and was content to say that religion helps "society" to control its members. With that, he severed the analysis of social control from the question of who controls whom. True, religion can make men perceive society as something more than the social relations and patterns of action that make it up, and thus it can act as a powerful legitimizing force. But too many studies of revivals perform the same function. Analyses of revivals and social control must not simply repeat that "religion" holds "society" together. They must define the ways in which particular religious beliefs reinforce the dominance of particular ruling groups.

The Rochester revival served the needs not of "society" but of entrepreneurs who employed wage labor. And while there are few systematic studies of revivals in other cities, there is reason to believe that the Rochester case was not unique. In towns and cities all over the northern United States, revivals after 1825 were tied closely to the growth of a manufacturing economy. Whitney Cross, in his pathbreaking study *The Burned-Over District*, found that revivals were strong in such manufacturing centers as Rochester, Lockport, and Utica, while the commercial centers of Buffalo and Albany remained quiet. Subsequent studies have reinforced his observation. Canal towns that were devoted to commerce were relatively immune to revivals. So were the old seaport cities. But in mill villages and manufacturing cities, evangelicalism struck as hard as it had at Rochester. The relation between revivals and manufactures gains strength when we turn from cities to individuals, for in urban places of all types, revivals and their related social movements were disproportionately strong among master workmen, manufacturers, and journeyman craftsmen. There were relatively few merchants and clerks among the converts, and even fewer day laborers and transport workers. Clearly, urban revivals in the 1820s and 1830s had something to do with the growth of manufactures.

In the few towns that have been studied over time, revivals followed the same chronology and served the same functions as they had at Rochester. Everywhere, enthusiasm struck first among masters and manufacturers, then spread through them into the ranks of labor. The workingman's revival of the 1830s was effected through missionary churches, temperance and moral reform societies, and Sunday schools that were dominated by rich evangelicals. The religion that it preached was order-inducing, repressive, and quintessentially bourgeois. In no city is there evidence of independent working-class revivals before the economic collapse of 1837. We must conclude that many workmen (the number varied enormously from town to town) were adopting the religion of the middle class, thus internalizing beliefs and modes of comportment that suited the needs of their employers.

The analysis of Rochester, along with evidence from other cities, allows us to hypothesize the social functions of urban revivals with some precision. Evangelicalism was a middle-class solution to problems of class, legitimacy, and order generated in the early stages of manufacturing. Revivals provided entrepreneurs with a means of imposing new standards of work discipline and personal comportment upon themselves and the men who worked for them, and thus they functioned as powerful social controls. But there was more to it than that. For the belief that every man was spiritually free and self-governing enabled masters to present a relationship that denied human interdependence as the realization of Christian ideals. Here we arrive at the means by which revivals served the needs of "society." For we have begun to define the role of religious sanctions in the process whereby a particular historical form of domination could assume legitimacy, and thus could indeed come to be perceived as "society." A significant minority of workingmen participated willingly in that process. And that, of course, is the most total and effective social control of all.

This solves the first problem raised by Tocqueville's analysis, but it confronts us with a second: the tendency to deduce the origins of religion from its social functions. Tocqueville stated that religion was strong in America because it created order among free individuals. . . . [R]evivals did indeed create order, but only along lines prescribed by an emerging industrial bourgeoisie. Here we enter dangerous territory. For if we infer the causes of revivals from their results, we must conclude that entrepreneurs consciously fabricated a religion that suited their economic and social needs. That would demonstrate little more than our own incapacity to take religion seriously. True, Charles Finney's revival at Rochester helped to solve the problems of labor discipline and social control in a new manufacturing city. But it was a religious solution, addressed to religious problems. The revival will remain unexplained until we know how social problems became translated into specifically religious unrest.

The businessmen and masters in Charles Finney's audience had been born into New England villages in which the roles of husband, father, and employer were intertwined, and they had reconstructed that village order on the banks of the Genesee [River flowing through Rochester]. In the early years, disorder and insubordination were held in check, for master and wage earner worked together and slept under the same roof. Fights between workmen were rare, and when they occurred masters witnessed the intelligible and personal stream of events that led up to them. Wage earners loafed or drank or broke the Sabbath only with the master's knowledge and tacit consent. When workers lived with proprietors or within sight of them, serious breaches of the peace or of accepted standards of labor discipline were uncommon. At the very least, workingmen were constrained to act like guests, and masters enforced order easily, in the course of ordinary social and economic transactions.

In the few years preceding the revival of 1831, Charles Finney's converts dissolved those arrangements. And as many recent studies have pointed out, that dissolution posed immense problems of work discipline and social order. In the experience of the master, however, it was worse than that. For when a master broke with home-centered relations of production he abdicated his authority as head of a household and as moral governor of society, and thus lost contact with a crucial part of his own identity. Given the money he made and the trouble he caused others, we need not sympathize too much. But if we are to render his turn to religion intelligible, we must understand that he experienced disobedience and disorder as religious problems— problems that had to do not only with safe streets and the efficient production of flour and shoes but with the "rightness" of new relations of production.

It was a dilemma that had no earthly solution. Rochester masters assumed the responsibility to govern wage earners. But at the same time they severed the relationships through which they had always dominated those men. Resistance in the workshops, the failure of the temperance crusade, and the results of elections in the 1820s dramatized what had become an everyday fact of life: workmen no longer listened when proprietors spoke. The authority of Rochester's ruling groups fell away, leaving them with new economic imperatives, old moral responsibilities, and no familiar and legitimate means of carrying them out. Attempts by a minority to reassert control through coercive means failed and, in the course of failing, split the elite and rendered concerted action impossible. It was the moral dilemma of free labor [the emerging notion that a worker's labor was a commodity to be sold as he or she saw fit] and the political impasse that it created that prepared the ground for Charles Finney.

The revival of 1831 healed divisions within the middle class and turned businessmen and masters into an active and united missionary army. Governing their actions in the 1830s was the new and reassuring knowledge that authoritarian controls were not necessary. For Finney had told them that man is not innately corrupt but only corruptible. There was no need to hold employees or anyone else in relations of direct dependence. Such relations, in fact, prevented underlings from discovering the infinite potential for good that was in each of them. Thus they inhibited individual conversion and blocked the millennium. From 1831 onward, middle-class religion in Rochester aimed not at the government of a sinful mankind but at the conversion of sinners and the perfection of the world.

The missions were a grand success: hundreds of wage earners joined middle-class churches in the 1830s. This pious enclave within the working class provided masters with more than willing workers and votes for Whig repression. Sober, hardworking, and obedient, they won the friendship and patronage of the middle class, and a startling number of them seized opportunities to become masters themselves. These men demonstrated that paternalistic controls could indeed be replaced by piety and voluntary self-restraint: free labor could generate a well-regulated, orderly, just, and happy society. The only thing needed was more revivals of religion. Workmen who continued to drink and carouse and stay away from church were no longer considered errant children; they were free moral agents who had chosen to oppose the Coming Kingdom. They could be hired when they were needed, fired without a qualm when they were not.

Thus a nascent industrial capitalism became attached to visions of a perfect moral order based on individual freedom and self-government, and old relations of dependence, servility, and mutuality were defined as sinful and left behind. The revival was not a capitalist plot. But it certainly was a crucial step in the legitimation of free labor.

The Democratization of American Christianity
Nathan O. Hatch

The wave of popular religious movements that broke upon the United States in the half century after independence did more to Christianize American society than anything before or since. Nothing makes that point more clearly than the growth of [evangelical] Methodist and Baptist movements among white and black Americans. Starting from scratch just prior to the Revolution, Methodism in America grew at a rate that terrified other more established denominations. By 1820 Methodist membership numbered a quarter million; by 1830 [near the height of the Second Great Awakening] it was twice that number. Baptist membership multiplied tenfold in the three decades after the Revolution; the number of churches increased from five hundred to over twenty-five hundred. The black church in Amer-

From Nathan O. Hatch, *The Democratization of American Christianity* (New Haven, CT: Yale University Press, 1989), 3-5, 9-11. Reprinted with permission.

ica was born amidst the crusading vigor of these movements and quickly assumed its own distinct character and broad appeal. By the middle of the nineteenth century, Methodist and Baptist churches had splintered into a score of separate denominations, white and black. In total, these movements eventually constituted two-thirds of the protestant ministers and church members in the United States.

Between the American Revolution and 1845, the population of the United States grew at a staggering rate: two and a half million became twenty million in seventy years. This unprecedented growth was due to a high birth rate and the availability of land, rather than to heavy immigration. . . .

Amidst this population boom, American Christianity became a mass enterprise. The eighteen hundred Christian ministers serving in 1775 swelled to nearly forty thousand by 1845. The number of preachers per capita more than tripled; the colonial legacy of one minister per fifteen hundred inhabitants became one per five hundred. This greater preaching density was remarkable given the spiraling population and the restless movement of peoples to occupy land beyond the reach of any church organization. The sheer number of new preachers was not a predictable outgrowth of religious conditions in the British colonies. Rather, their sudden growth indicated a profound religious upsurge and resulted in a vastly altered religious landscape. Twice the number of denominations competed for adherents, and insurgents often enjoyed the upper hand. . . .

This book examines five distinct traditions, or mass movements, that developed early in the nineteenth century: the Christian movement, the Methodists, the Baptists, the black churches, and the Mormons. Each was led by young men of relentless energy who went about movement-building as self-conscious outsiders. They shared an ethic of unrelenting toil, a passion for expansion, a hostility to orthodox belief and style, a zeal for religious reconstruction, and a systematic plan to realize their ideals. However diverse their theologies and church organizations, they all offered common people, especially the poor, compelling visions of individual self-respect and collective self-confidence. Like the Populist movement at the end of the nineteenth century, these movements took shape around magnetic leaders who were highly skilled in communication and group mobilization.

Abstractions and generalities about the Second Great Awakening as a conservative force have obscured the egalitarianism powerfully at work in the new nation. As common people became significant actors on the religious scene, there was increasing confusion and angry debate over the purpose and function of the church. A style of religious leadership that the public deemed "untutored" and "irregular" as late as the First Great Awakening [from the 1740s to the 1770s] became overwhelmingly successful, even normative, in the first decades of the republic. Ministers from different classes vied with each other to serve as divine spokesmen. Democratic or populist leaders associated virtue with ordinary people and exalted the vernacular [common way of speaking] in word, print, and song. . . .

Religious populism has been a residual agent of change in America over the last two centuries, an inhibitor of genteel tradition and a recurring source of new religious movements. Deep and powerful undercurrents of democratic Christianity distinguish the United States from other modern industrial democracies. These currents insure that churches in this land do not withhold faith from the rank and file. Instead, religious leaders have pursued people wherever they could be found; embraced them without regard to social standing; and challenged them to think, to interpret Scripture, and to organize the church for themselves. Religious populism, reflecting the passions of ordinary people and the charisma of democratic movement-builders, remains among the oldest and deepest impulses in American life. . . .

America's nonrestrictive environment permitted an unexpected and often explosive conjunction of evangelical fervor and popular sovereignty. It was this engine that accelerated the process of Christianization within American popular culture, allowing indigenous expressions of faith to take hold among ordinary people, white and black. This expansion of evangelical Christianity did not proceed primarily from the nimble response of religious elites meeting the challenge before them. Rather, Christianity was effectively reshaped by common people who molded it in their own image and who threw themselves into expanding its influence. Increasingly assertive common people wanted their leaders unpretentious, their doctrines self-evident and down-to-earth, their music lively and singable, and their churches in local hands. It was this upsurge of democratic hope that characterized so many religious cultures in the early republic and brought Baptists, Methodists, Disciples of Christ, and a host of other insurgent groups to the fore. The rise of evangelical Christianity in the early republic is, in some measure, a story of the success of common people in shaping the culture after their own priorities rather than the priorities outlined by gentlemen such as the framers of the Constitution.

It is easy to miss the democratic character of the early republic's insurgent religious movements. The Methodists, after all, retained power in a structured hierarchy under the control of bishops. The Mormons reverted to rule by a single religious prophet and revelator. And groups such as the Disciples of Christ, despite professed democratic structures, were eventually controlled by such powerful individuals as Alexander Campbell, who had little patience with dissent. As ecclesiastical structures, these movements often turned out to be less democratic than [earlier American congregations]. The rise of popular sovereignty . . . often has involved insurgent leaders glorifying the many as a way to legitimate their own authority.

The democratization of Christianity, then, has less to do with the specifics of polity and governance and more with the incarnation of the church into popular culture. In at least three respects the popular religious movements of the early republic articulated a profoundly democratic spirit. First, they denied the age-old distinction that set the clergy apart as a separate order of men, and they refused to defer to learned theologians and traditional orthodoxies. All were democratic or populist in the way they instinctively associated virtue with ordinary people rather than with elites, exalted the vernacular in word and song as the hallowed channel for communicating with and about God, and freely turned over the reigns of power. These groups also shared with the Jeffersonian Republicans an overt rejection of the past as a repository of wisdom. By redefining leadership itself, these movements reconstructed the foundations of religion in keeping with the values and priorities of ordinary people.

Second, these movements empowered ordinary people by taking their deepest spiritual impulses at face value rather than subjecting them to the scrutiny of orthodox doctrine and the frowns of respectable clergymen. In the last two decades of the century, preachers from a wide range of new religious movements openly fanned the flames of religious ecstasy. Rejecting the Yankee Calvinism of his youth in 1775, Henry Alline found that his soul was transported with divine love, "ravished with a divine ecstasy beyond any doubts or fears, or thoughts of being then deceived." What had been defined as "enthusiasm" was increasingly advocated from the pulpit as an essential part of Christianity. Such a shift in emphasis, accompanied by rousing gospel singing rather than formal church music, reflected the common people's success in defining the nature of faith for themselves. In addition, an unprecedented wave of religious leaders in the last quarter of the eighteenth century expressed their openness to a variety of signs and wonders, in short, an admission of increased supernatural involvement in everyday life. Scores of preachers' journals, from Methodists and Baptists, from north and south, from white and black, indicated a ready acceptance to consider dreams and visions as inspired by God, normal manifestations of divine guidance and instruction. "I know the word of God is our infallible guide, and by it we are to try all our dreams and feelings," conceded the Methodist stalwart Freeborn Garrettson. But he added, "I also know, that both sleeping and waking, things of a divine nature have been revealed to me." Volatile aspects of popular region, long held in check by the church, were recognized and encouraged from the pulpit. It is no wonder that a dismayed writer in the *Connecticut Evangelical Magazine* countered in 1805: "No person is warranted from the word of God to publish to the world the discoveries of heaven or hell which he supposes he has had in a dream, or trance, or vision."

The early republic was also a democratic movement in a third sense. Religious outsiders, flushed with confidence about their prospects, had little sense of their limitations. They dreamed that a new age of religious and social harmony would naturally spring up out of their efforts to overthrow coercive and authoritarian structures. This upsurge of democratic hope, this passion for equality, led to a welter of diverse and competing forms, many of them structured in highly undemocratic ways. The Methodists under Francis Asbury, for instance, used authoritarian means to build a church that would not be a respecter of persons. This church faced the curious paradox of gaining phenomenal influence among laypersons with whom it would not share ecclesiastical authority. Similarly, the Mormons used a virtual religious dictatorship as the means to return power to illiterate men. Yet despite these authoritarian structures, the fundamental impetus of these movements was to make Christianity a liberating force; people were given the right to think and act for themselves rather than depending upon the mediations of an educated elite. The most fascinating religious story of the early republic is the signal achievements of these and other populist religious leaders—outsiders who used democratic persuasions to reconstruct the foundations of religious authority.

Questions for Discussion

1. Are religious revivals simply a product of the mysterious workings of faith, or do certain social factors determine their success or failure? Do revivals promote democracy, or is religion a mechanism of social control? Which, if either, of the above explanations of religious revivalism do you find more convincing? Are they mutually exclusive?

2. How has religion shaped American history? What connections do you see between the revivalism and reform of the Second Great Awakening and the larger social changes that took place between the Revolution and the Civil War?

3. Is religion as influential in the United States today as it was during the Second Great Awakening? In what ways does religion affect modern American society?

5

War With Mexico

Guerra, Gold, and Slaves: Why did the United States Go to War with Mexico?

In January 1848 a freshman congressman from Illinois named Abraham Lincoln (then a member of the Whig party) publicly questioned President James K. Polk's motives for leading the country to war against Mexico. At Polk's urging, Congress had voted overwhelmingly in May 1846 to declare war on its neighbor to the south. By September of the following year the Stars and Stripes flew over the Mexican National Palace. Although Polk claimed that U.S. troops had been attacked on their own soil and thus had the right to defend the nation from Mexican hostility, the reality is that the president ordered the army into provocative positions within disputed territory until the Mexican military responded. It does not take a stretch of the imagination to see the war with Mexico as America's first war of aggression, in which the United States was the antagonist rather than the defender. That is exactly how many people saw it at the time, including writer Henry David Thoreau, who joined Lincoln in condemning the war as unjustified and (according to a Congressional resolution) "unnecessarily and unconstitutionally commenced by the President."

These protests did not appreciably impact the war effort, and on February 2, 1848, commissioners from the Mexican government met with an unauthorized agent of the State Department at the Villa de Guadalupe Hildalgo, only a short distance north of the Mexican capital. Across from a shrine to the Virgen de Guadalupe, the patron saint of Mexico, these negotiators signed a treaty that would bring an end to the war. According to the terms of the Treaty of Guadalupe Hidalgo, Mexico ceded 55 percent of its territory to the invader in exchange for $15 million and the assumption of more than $3 million in debts owed to United States citizens. The surrendered land encompassed most of the present-day Southwest, including all or part of the states of California, Arizona, New Mexico, Nevada, Utah, Colorado, Wyoming, and a small corner of Kansas, as well as claims to Texas above the Rio Grande (the original disputed territory). People living in these areas—roughly 100,000 Mexican citizens and unknown numbers of Indians—went to sleep in Mexico one night and woke up in the United States the next morning. The victorious republic saw the continent open up before it, its "Manifest Destiny" to span the land from Atlantic to Pacific now clearly within reach.

Yet even before the treaty was signed, both Northerners and Southerners also saw the catch to such extraordinary expansion: The addition of such a vast new territory raised urgent questions about the future of slavery and whether it should be allowed to expand. And there was another double-edged blessing hidden in the newly acquired land: Not two weeks before the treaty was signed, gold had been discovered at Sutter's Mill in California. Neither government was aware of it at the time, but when news of the strike finally reached the states it was clear that, from a financial perspective, the nation had made an astonishingly good deal—perhaps good enough to overwhelm objections to the war and, in some minds, justify the taking. Western gold poured into the financial centers of the Northeast, providing capital to accelerate the region's shift toward industrialization while the South remained largely agrarian. Throughout the following decade these divergent (but potentially complementary) economic outlooks, combined with skirmishes over slavery, added to the growing tension between North and South, and when fighting finally erupted between the states, many Americans viewed the conflict with Mexico as the tipping point that had set the nation on the course to Civil War.

War Message to Congress
James K. Polk

Washington, May 11, 1846

To the Senate and House of Representatives:

The existing state of the relations between the United States and Mexico renders it proper that I should bring the subject to the consideration of Congress. In my message at the commencement of your present session the state of these relations; the causes which led to the suspension of diplomatic intercourse between the two countries in March, 1845, and the long-continued and unredressed wrongs and injuries committed by the Mexican Government on citizens of the United States in their persons and property were briefly set forth.

As the facts and opinions which were then laid before you were care fully considered, I can not better express my present convictions of the condition of affairs up to that time than by referring you to that communication.

The strong desire to establish peace with Mexico on liberal and honorable terms, and the readiness of this Government to regulate and adjust our boundary and other causes of difference with that power on such fair and equitable principles as would lead to permanent relations of the most friendly nature, induced me in September last to seek the reopening of diplomatic relations between the two countries. Every measure adopted on our part had for its object the furtherance of these desired results. In communicating to Congress a succinct statement of the injuries which we had suffered from Mexico, and which have been accumulating during a period of more than twenty years, every expression that could tend to inflame the people of Mexico or defeat or delay a pacific result was carefully avoided. An envoy of the United States repaired to Mexico with full powers to adjust every existing difference. But though present on the Mexican soil by agreement between the two Governments, invested with full powers, and bearing evidence of the most friendly dispositions, his mission has been unavailing. The Mexican Government not only refused to receive him or listen to his propositions, but after a long-continued series of menaces have at last invaded our territory and shed the blood of our fellow-citizens on our own soil. . . .

The Mexican forces at Matamoras assumed a belligerent attitude,

From James K. Polk, "Message to Congress," in James D. Richardson, ed., *A Compilation of the Messages and Papers of the Presidents*, vol. 4 (Washington, D.C.: 1903), 440-3.

and on the 12th of April General Ampudia, then in command, notified General Taylor to break up his camp within twenty-four hours and to retire beyond the Nueces River, and in the event of his failure to comply with these demands announced that arms, and arms alone, must decide the question. But no open act of hostility was committed until the 14th of April. On that day General Arista, who had succeeded to the command of the Mexican forces, communicated to General Taylor that he considered hostilities commenced and should prosecute them. A party of dragoons of 63 men and officers were on the same day dispatched from the American camp up the Rio del Norte, on its left bank, to ascertain whether the Mexican troops had crossed or were preparing to cross the river, became engaged with a large body of these troops, and after a short affair, in which some 16 were killed and wounded, appear to have been surrounded and compelled to surrender. The grievous wrongs perpetrated by Mexico upon our citizens throughout a long period of years remain unredressed, and solemn treaties pledging her public faith for this redress have been disregarded. A government either unable or unwilling to enforce the execution of such treaties fails to perform one of its plainest duties.

Our commerce with Mexico has been almost annihilated. It was formerly highly beneficial to both nations, but our merchants have been deterred from prosecuting it by the system of outrage and extortion which the Mexican authorities have pursued against them, whilst their appeals through their own Government for indemnity have been made in vain. Our forbearance has gone to such an extreme as to be mistaken in its character. Had we acted with vigor in repelling the insults and redressing the injuries inflicted by Mexico at the commencement, we should doubtless have escaped all the difficulties in which we are now involved.

Instead of this, however, we have been exerting our best efforts to propitiate her good will. Upon the pretext that Texas, a nation as independent as herself, thought proper to unite its destinies with our own she has affected to believe that we have severed her rightful territory, and in official proclamations and manifestoes has repeatedly threatened to make war upon us for the purpose of reconquering Texas. In the meantime we have tried every effort at reconciliation. The cup of forbearance had been exhausted even before the recent information from the frontier of the Del Norte. But now, after reiterated menaces, Mexico has passed the boundary of the United States, has invaded our territory and shed American blood upon the American soil. She has proclaimed that hostilities have commenced, and that the two nations are now at war.

As war exists, and, notwithstanding all our efforts to avoid it, exists by the act of Mexico herself, we are called upon by every consideration of duty and patriotism to vindicate with decision the honor, the rights, and the interests of our country.

Speech in the United States House of Representatives
Abraham Lincoln

January 12, 1848

When the war began, it was my opinion that all those who because of knowing too little, or because of knowing too much, could not conscientiously oppose the conduct of the President in the beginning of it should nevertheless, as good citizens and patriots, remain silent on that point, at least till the war should be ended. Some leading Democrats, including ex-President Van Buren, have taken this same view, as I understand them; and I adhered to it and acted upon it, until since I took my seat here; and I think I should still adhere to it were it not that the President and his friends will not allow it to be so. Besides the continual effort of the President to argue every silent vote given for supplies into an indorsement of the Justice and wisdom of his conduct; besides that singularly candid paragraph in his late message in which he tells us that Congress with great unanimity had declared that "by the act of the Republic of Mexico, a state of war exists between that Government and the United States," when the same Journals that informed him of this also informed him that when that declaration stood disconnected from the question of supplies sixty-seven in the House, and not fourteen merely, voted against it; besides this open attempt to prove by telling the truth what he could no [sic] prove by telling the whole truth—demanding of all who will not submit to be misrepresented, in justice to themselves, to speak out,—besides all this, one of my colleagues [Mr. Richardson] at a very early day in the session brought in a set of resolutions expressly indorsing the original justice of the war on the part of the President. Upon these resolutions when they shall be put on their passage I shall be compelled to vote; so that I cannot be silent if I would. Seeing this, I went about preparing myself to give the vote understandingly when it should come. I carefully examined the President's message, to ascer-

From Abraham Lincoln, "Speech in the United States House of Representatives, January 12, 1848," in John G. Nicolay and John Hay, eds., *The Complete Works of Abraham Lincoln*, vol. 1 (New York: Francis D. Tandy Company, 1894), 328-30, 337-45.

tain what he himself had said and proved upon the point. The result of this examination was to make the impression that, taking for true all the President states as facts, he falls far short of proving his justification; and that the President would have gone farther with his proof if it had not been for the small matter that the truth would not permit him. Under the impression thus made I gave the vote before mentioned. I propose now to give concisely the process of the examination I made, and how I reached the conclusion I did. The President, in his first war message of May, 1846, declares that the soil was ours on which hostilities were commenced by Mexico, and he repeats that declaration almost in the same language in each successive annual message, thus showing that he deems that point a highly essential one. In the importance of that point I entirely agree with the President. To my judgment it is the very point upon which he should be justified, or condemned. In his message of December, 1846, it seems to have occurred to him, as is certainly true, that title—ownership— to soil or anything else is not a simple fact, but is a conclusion following on one or more simple facts; and that it was incumbent upon him to present the facts from which he concluded the soil was ours on which the first blood of the war was shed. . . .

I am now through the whole of the President's evidence; and it is a singular fact that if any one should declare the President sent the army into the midst of a settlement of Mexican people who had never submitted, by consent or by force, to the authority of Texas or of the United States, and that there and thereby the first blood of the war was shed, there is not one word in all the President has said which would either admit or deny the declaration. This strange omission it does seem to me could not have occurred but by design. My way of living leads me to be about the courts of justice; and there I have sometimes seen a good lawyer, struggling for his client's neck in a desperate case, employing every artifice to work round, befog, and cover up with many words some point arising in the case which he dared not admit and yet could not deny. Party bias may help to make it appear so, but with all the allowance I can make for such bias, it still does appear to me that just such, and from just such necessity, is the President's struggle in this case.

Some time after my colleague [Mr. Richardson] introduced the resolutions I have mentioned, I introduced a preamble, resolution, and interrogations, intended to draw the President out, if possible, on this hitherto untrodden ground. To show their relevancy, I propose to state my understanding of the true rule for ascertaining the boundary between Texas and Mexico. It is that wherever Texas was exercising jurisdiction was hers; and wherever Mexico was exercising jurisdiction was hers; and that whatever separated the actual exercise of jurisdiction of the one from that of the other was the true boundary between them. If, as is probably true, Texas was exercising jurisdiction along the western bank of the Nueces, and Mexico was exercising it along the eastern bank of the Rio Grande, then neither river was the boundary; but the uninhabited country between the two was. The extent of our territory in that region depended not on any treaty-fixed boundary (for no treaty had attempted it), but on revolution. Any people anywhere being inclined and having the power have the right to rise up and shake off the existing government, and form a new one that suits them better. This is a most valuable, a most sacred right—a right which we hope and believe is to liberate the world. Nor is this right confined to cases in which the whole people of an existing government may choose to exercise it. Any portion of such people that can may revolutionize and make their own of so much of the territory as they inhabit. More than this, a majority of any portion of such people may revolutionize, putting down a minority, intermingled with or near about them, who may oppose this movement. Such minority was precisely the case of the Tories of our own revolution. It is a quality of revolutions not to go by old lines or old laws; but to break up both, and make new ones.

As to the country now in question, we bought it of France in 1803, and sold it to Spain in 1819, according to the President's statements. After this, all Mexico, including Texas, revolutionized against Spain; still later Texas revolutionized against Mexico. In my view, just so far as she carried her resolution by obtaining the actual, willing or unwilling, submission of the people, so far the country was hers, and no farther. Now, sir, for the purpose of obtaining the very best evidence as to whether Texas had actually carried her revolution to the place where the hostilities of the present war commenced, let the President answer the interrogatories I proposed, as before mentioned, or some other similar ones. Let him answer fully, fairly, and candidly. Let him answer with facts and not with arguments. Let him remember he sits where Washington sat, and so remembering, let him answer as Washington would answer. As a nation should not, and the Almighty will not, be evaded, so let him attempt no evasion—no equivocation. And if, so answering, he can show that the soil was ours where the first blood of the war was shed,—that it was not within an inhabited country, or, if within such, that the inhabitants had submitted themselves to the civil authority of Texas or of the United States, and that the same is true of the site of Fort Brown,—then I am with him for his justification. In that case I shall be most happy to reverse the vote I gave the other day. I have a selfish motive for desiring that the President may do this—I expect to gain some votes, in connection with the war, which, without his so doing, will be of doubtful propriety in my own Judgment, but which will be free from the doubt if he does so. But if he can not or will not do this,—if on any pretense or no pretense he shall refuse or omit it—then I shall be fully convinced of what I more than suspect already—that he is deeply conscious of being in the wrong; that he feels the blood of this war, like the blood of Abel, is crying to Heaven against him; that originally having some strong motive—what, I will not stop now to give my opinion concerning—to involve the two countries in a war, and trusting to escape scrutiny by fixing the public gaze upon the exceeding brightness of military glory,—that attractive rainbow that arises in showers of blood—that serpent's eye that charms to destroy,—he plunged into it, and has swept on and on till, disappointed in his calculation of the ease with which Mexico might be subdued, he now finds himself he knows not where. How like the half-insane mumbling of a fever dream is the whole war part of his late message! . . .

The war has gone on some twenty months; for the expenses of which, together with an inconsiderable old score, the President now claims about one half of the Mexican territory, and that by far the better half, so far as concerns our ability to make anything out of it. It is comparatively uninhabited, so that we could establish land offices in it, and raise some money in that way. But the other half is already inhabited, as I understand it, tolerably densely for the nature of the country, and all its lands, or all that are valuable, already appropriated as private property. How then are we to make anything out of these lands with this encumbrance upon them? or how remove the encumbrance? I suppose no one would say we should kill the people, or drive them out, or make slaves of them; or confiscate their property. How, then, can we make much out of this part of the territory? If the prosecution of the war has in expenses already equaled the better half of the country, how long its future prosecution will be in equaling the less valuable half is not a speculative, but a practical, question, pressing closely upon us. And yet it is a question which the President seems never to have thought of. As to the mode of terminating the war and securing peace, the President is equally wandering and indefinite. First, it is to be done by a more vigorous prosecution of the war in the vital parts of the enemy's country; and after apparently talking himself tired on this point, the President drops down into a half-despairing tone, and tells us that "with a people distracted and divided by contending factions, and a government subject to constant changes by successive revolutions, the continued success of our arms may fail to secure a satisfactory peace." Then he suggests the propriety of wheedling the Mexican people to desert the counsels of their own leaders, and, trusting in our protestations, to set up a government from which we can secure a satisfactory peace; telling us that "this may become the only mode of obtaining such a peace." But soon he falls into a doubt of this too; and then drops back onto the already half-abandoned ground of "more vigorous prosecution." All this shows that the President is in nowise satisfied with his own positions. First he takes up one, and in attempting to argue us into it he argues himself out of it, then seizes another and goes through the same process, and then, confused at being able to think of nothing new, he snatches up the old one again, which he has some time before cast off. His mind, taxed beyond its power, is running hither and thither, like some tortured creature on a burning surface, finding no position on which it can settle down and be at ease.

Again, it is a singular omission in this message that it nowhere intimates when the President expects the war to terminate. At its beginning, General Scott was by this same President driven into disfavor, if not disgrace, for intimating that peace could not be conquered in less than three or four months. But now, at the end of about twenty months, during which time our arms have given us the most splendid successes, every department and every part, land and water, officers and privates, regulars and volunteers, doing all that men could do, and hundreds of things which it had ever before been thought men could not do—after all this, this same President gives us a long message, without showing us that as to the end he himself has even an imaginary conception. As I have before said, he knows not where he is. He is a bewildered, confounded, and miserably perplexed man. God grant he may be able to show there is not something about his conscience more painful than all his mental perplexity.

Questions for Discussion

1. Was the United States justified in going to war with Mexico? In taking so much land in the peace settlement?

2. In what ways did the acquisition of the Mexican lands benefit the nation? What negative impacts did it have? Is it possible, or useful, to characterize historical events as positive or negative? When, if ever, should historians make such judgments about the past, and what criteria should they consider?

3. Did the questions about slavery prompted by the war with Mexico make the Civil War inevitable?

4. Is dissent unpatriotic in wartime? What, if anything, does it achieve? What are the limits of acceptable protest?

6

The Civil War

Massa Lincoln? Was the Great Emancipator a White Supremacist?

For many people, Abraham Lincoln's lean, introspective countenance personifies both the tragedy and the hope of the Civil War. Traditionally, he has been celebrated by black and white Americans alike as the Great Emancipator, the man who abolished slavery and brought freedom to blacks throughout the Union. But Lincoln was a complex man navigating one of the most difficult times in the nation's history, and his words and actions were broad enough to accommodate many other interpretations. Lerone Bennett, Jr., a historian and the executive editor emeritus of *Ebony* magazine, argues that Lincoln shared the racist views of his time and that only the demands of the war forced the reluctant president to choose emancipation. Lincoln biographer Stephen B. Oates disputes this revisionist portrait, insisting that Lincoln despised slavery and, once conditions had persuaded him, threw the full force of his presidential power behind partial and then total abolition.

The Civil War did not just abolish slavery—in a broader sense, it tried and tempered the ideals that the nation had proclaimed at its origin. The Declaration of Independence had declared that "all men are created equal," but the Constitution had enshrined the right to own slaves among the liberties enjoyed by Americans. The slender threads that held such a paradox together came unraveled with the succession of eleven Southern states in 1860 and 1861, and Lincoln was charged with restoring the Union whole again.

Against the backdrop of a brutal and prolonged war, he weighed the military and moral arguments for emancipation against legal, political, and perhaps personal reservations.

The course that Lincoln finally chose reconfigured the meaning of the war and committed the nation forever after (in principle) to expanding the sphere of liberty. The Emancipation Proclamation has become a touchstone for those who feel that the United States has a moral obligation to advance freedom and equality through-out the nation and the world. Lincoln has been memorialized on the national mall in Washington, D.C., honored on the country's currency, and even had his likeness carved into a mountainside. Yet all too often, this admiration for his decision to free the slaves obscures the story of his struggle and hesitation with the question. Does reconsidering the motives for his greatest act jeopardize his standing among America's finest leaders? Do his complex views taint the worthiness of his actions? Are complicated heroes less heroic?

Was Abe Lincoln a White Supremacist?
Lerone Bennett, Jr.

Abraham Lincoln was *not* the Great Emancipator. As we shall see, there is abundant evidence to indicate that the Emancipation Procla-mation was not what people think it is and that Lincoln issued it with extreme misgivings and reservations. Even more decisive is the fact that the real Lincoln was a tragically flawed figure who shared the racial prejudices of most of his white contemporaries. . . .

In the general literature, Lincoln is depicted as an eloquent and flaming idealist, whaling away at the demon of slavery. This view is almost totally false. In the first place, Lincoln was an opportunist, not an idealist. He was a man of the fence, a man of the middle, a man who stated the principle with great eloquence but almost always shied away from rigid commitments to practice. Contrary to reports, Lin-coln was no social revolutionary. As a matter of fact, he was an ar-chetypal example of the cautious politician who assails the extrem-ists on both sides. It is not for nothing that cautious politicians sing his praises.

It should be noted, secondly, that Lincoln's position on slavery has been grossly misrepresented. Lincoln was not opposed to slavery; he

From Lerone Bennett, Jr., "Was Abe Lincoln a White Supremacist?" *Ebony* 24, no. 4 (Feb 1968): 35-42. Reprinted with permission.

was opposed to the *extension* of slavery. More than that: Lincoln was opposed to the extension of slavery out of devotion to the interests of white people, not out of compassion for suffering blacks. To be sure, he did say from time to time that slavery was "a monstrous injustice." But he also said, repeatedly, that he was not prepared to do anything to remove that injustice where it existed. On the contrary, he said that it was his duty to tolerate and, if necessary, to give practical support to an evil supported by the U.S. Constitution. . . .

Lincoln came down off the fence, rhetorically, in the '50s when the Kansas-Nebraska act reopened the whole question of the extension of slavery to the largely uninhabited territories of the West. This was, he said, a clear and present threat to free white men and to what he called "the white man's charter of freedom"—the Declaration of Independence. In his public speeches of this period, Lincoln was given to saying in the same speech that he believed in white supremacy as a practical matter and in the Declaration of Independence as an abstract matter of principle.

The Lincoln years in Illinois were years of oppression and reaction. Black people could not vote, testify against white people in court or attend public schools. It was a crime for free black people to settle in the state. Although Lincoln was a powerful figure in state politics for more than a quarter of a century, he made no audible protest against this state of affairs. In fact, he said he preferred it that way. When H. Ford Douglas, a militant black leader, asked Lincoln to support a movement to repeal the law banning black testimony, Lincoln refused.

In the famous series of debates with Stephen Douglas, Lincoln made his position crystal clear. He was opposed, he said, to Negro citizenship and to "the niggers and the white people marrying together." Speaking at Charleston, Illinois on September 18, 1858, Lincoln said: "I will say, then, that I am not, nor ever have been, in favor of bringing about in any way the social and political equality of the white and black races; (applause) that I am not, nor ever have been, in favor of making voters or jurors of Negroes, nor of qualifying them to hold office, nor to intermarry with white people; and I will say, in addition, to this, that there is a physical difference between the white and black races which I believe will forever forbid the two races living together on terms of social and political equality. And inasmuch as they cannot so live, while they do remain together there must be the position of superior and inferior, and I as much as any other man am in favor of having the superior position assigned to the white race.". . .

The traditional image of Lincoln is of a harried and large-hearted man fending off "extremists of the left and right" only to emerge at the precise psychological moment to do what he had always wanted to do. This image clashes, unfortunately, with the evidence which suggests that sudden and general emancipation was never Lincoln's policy.

Lincoln was given to saying that his constitutional duties prevented him from doing anything substantial to give point to his "oft-expressed *personal* wish that all men everywhere could be free." But it is obvious from the evidence that Lincoln's problems were deeper than that. For when his duty was clear, he refused to act. On several occasions he refused to take anti-slavery action which was mandated by Congress and he sabotaged some anti-slavery legislation by executive inaction. Somehow, duty, in Lincoln's view, almost always worked against the black man.

Lincoln defenders say that he resisted emancipation pressures because of his fear that premature action would alienate white supporters in Northern and Border States and endanger the prosecution of the war. But this view does not come to grips with the fact that Lincoln was *personally* opposed to sudden and general emancipation before 1861 and the further fact that he continued to oppose sudden and general emancipation after the circulating Proclamation proved his fears were groundless. Nor does the traditional Lincoln apologia touch the mass of evidence—in Lincoln letters as well as in private and public statements—which shows that Lincoln was personally opposed to sudden emancipation on social and racial grounds.

It was not the fear of emancipation but the fear of what would happen afterwards that palsied Lincoln's hands. He was deeply disturbed by the implications of turning loose four million black people in a land he considered the peculiar preserve of the white man. He spoke often of "the evils of sudden derangement" and warned Congress against "the vagrant destitution which must largely attend immediate emancipation in localities where their numbers are very great." He said over and over again that it was his considered judgment that "gradual, and not sudden, emancipation is better for all.". . .

An additional factor in Lincoln's opposition to the principle of sudden emancipation was his racial bias. He considered black people unassimilable aliens. There was not, in his view, enough room in America for black and white people. He didn't believe white people would sanction equal rights for black people and he didn't ask white people to sanction equal rights for black people. Since he did not propose to confront racism, he told black people they would have to travel or accept a subordinate position in American life.

Insofar as it can be said that Lincoln had an emancipation policy, it was to rid America of slaves and Negroes. When he failed in his attempt to end the war without touching slavery, he fell back to a second plan of gradual and compensated emancipation extending over a 37-year-period. This was linked in his thinking with a companion policy of colonizing black people in South America or Africa. . . .

While Lincoln was trying to send black people away, Congress was busy emancipating. In the spring and summer of 1862, Congress forbade military officers to return fugitive slaves, authorized the President to accept black soldiers, and emancipated the slaves in Washington D.C. Finally, on July 17, 1862, Congress passed the Second Confiscation Act, which freed the slaves of all rebels. This act, which has received insufficient attention in general media, was actually more sweeping than the preliminary Emancipation Proclamation, which came two months later.

Lincoln followed Congress' lead slowly and grudgingly, signing most of these acts with evident displeasure. But the drift of events was unmistakable, and Lincoln changed steps, saying with great honesty that he had not controlled events but had been controlled by them. Conferring with the member of a congressional committee charged with drafting a plan for buying the slaves and sending them away, Lincoln urged speed, saying: "You had better come to an agreement. Niggers will never be cheaper."

Orthography apart, Lincoln caught here the spirit of the times. At that moment, in late July of 1862, the Union war effort was bogged down in the marshes of Virginia, and England and France were on the verge of intervening on the side of the Confederacy. At home, the heat was rising fast, fueled by mounting Northern casualties. Faced with mushrooming pressures home and abroad, Lincoln reversed his course and "conditionally determined," to use his words, to touch the institution of slavery.

Lincoln adopted the new policy from necessity, not conviction. In public and in private, he made it clear that he was not motivated by compassion for the slaves. Taking his stand on the ground of military necessity, he said his new policy was designed to weaken Southern white men and to strengthen the hand of Northern white men. "Things," he said later, "had gone from bad to worse, till I felt we had reached the end of the rope on the plan of operation we had been pursuing, and that we had about played our last card." Lincoln said he was driven to the "alternative of either surrendering the Union, and with it, the Constitution, or of laying a strong hand upon the colored element."

There was truth in this, but it was not the whole truth. There is evidence that Lincoln was forced to adopt the new policy by political pressures. Edward Stanly, military governor of North Carolina, said Lincoln told him that "the proclamation had become a civil necessity to prevent the Radicals from openly embarrassing the government in the conduct of the war. The President expressed the belief that, without the proclamation for which they had been clamoring, the Radicals would take the extreme step in Congress of withholding supplies for carrying on the war—leaving the whole land in anarchy." Count [Adam] Gurowski gave a similar version of Lincoln's metamorphosis and concluded, in a fine phrase, that Lincoln was literally "whipped" into glory.

Responding to a parallelogram of pressures, Lincoln issued a preliminary Emancipation Proclamation on September 22, 1862. In this document, he warned the South that he would issue a final Emancipation Proclamation in 100 days if the rebellion had not ended by that time. The proclamation outlined a future policy of emancipation, but Lincoln had no joy in the black harvest. To a group of serenaders, who congratulated him on the new policy, Lincoln said: "I can only trust in God I have made no mistake." To his old friend Joshua F. Speed, Lincoln expressed misgivings and said he had "been anxious to avoid it." To Congressman John Convode of Pennsylvania, Lincoln explained that he had been *"driven to it,"* adding: "But although my duty is plain, it is in some respects painful. . . ." Still another visitor, Edward Stanly, received a dramatic account of Lincoln's resistance to a policy of emancipation. "Mr. Lincoln said," according to Stanly, "that he had prayed to the Almighty to save him from this necessity, adopting the very language of our Saviour. 'If it be possible, let this cup pass from me,' but the prayer had not been answered."

On Thursday, January 1, 1863, Lincoln drank from the cup, and apparently he liked neither the flavor nor the color of the draught. When he started to sign the document, his arm trembled so violently, an eyewitness said, that he could not hold the pen. Lincoln, who was very superstitious, paused, startled. Then, attributing his shakes to the hours of hand-shaking at a New Year's Day reception, he scrawled his name, saying he did not want the signature to be "tremulous" because people would say "he had some compunctions."

He had "compunctions."

Nothing indicates this better than the Emancipation Proclamation which is, as J. G. Randall and Richard N. Current indicated, "more often admired than read." Cold, forbidding, with all the moral grandeur of a real estate deed, the Proclamation does not enumerate a single principle hostile to slavery and it contains not one quotable sentence. As a document, it lends weight to the observation of Lincoln's law partner, William Herndon, who wrote: "When he freed the slaves, there was no heart in the act."

There wasn't much else in it, either. Rightly speaking, the Emancipation Proclamation, as Ralph Korngold wrote, was "not an Emancipation Proclamation at all." The document was drafted in such a way that it freed few, if any, slaves. It did not apply to slaves in the Border States and areas under federal control in the South. In other words, Lincoln "freed" slaves where he had no power and left them in chains where he had power. The theory behind the Proclamation, an English paper noted, "is not that a human being cannot justly own another, but that he cannot own him unless he is loyal to the United States."

The Proclamation argues so powerfully against itself that some scholars have suggested that Lincoln was trying to do the opposite of what he said he was doing. In other words, the suggestion is that the Emancipation Proclamation was a political stratagem by which Lincoln hoped to outflank the Radicals, buy time and forestall a definitive act of Emancipation. . . .

"The Man of Our Redemption"
Stephen B. Oates

In 1860, when he won the Republican nomination for President, Lincoln stood before the American electorate on the free-soil, free-labor principles of the Republican party. As the Republican standard bearer, Lincoln was uncompromising in his determination to prohibit slavery in the territories by national law and to save the Republic (as he put it) from returning "class, caste, and despotism." He exhorted his fellow Republicans to stand firm in their duty: if their position on slavery precipitated a crisis, it would have to be. Some day the American house must be free of human bondage. That was the Republican vision, the distant horizon Lincoln saw.

Yet for the benefit of southerners, he repeated that he and his party would not harm slavery in the southern states. The federal government had no constitutional authority in peacetime to menace a state institution like slavery.

But by 1860 southerners were in no mood to believe anything Lincoln or any other Republican said. In Dixie, orators and editors alike derided Lincoln as a black-hearted radical, a "sooty and scoundrelly" abolitionist who wanted to free the slaves at once and mix the races. By turns, southerners branded Lincoln as another John Brown, a mobocat, a southern hater, a chimpanzee, a lunatic, the "biggest ass in the United States," the evil chief of the North's "Black Republican, free love, free Nigger" party whose victory would ring the bells of

From Stephen B. Oates, "'The Man of Our Redemption:' Abraham Lincoln and the Emancipation of the Slaves," *Presidential Studies Quarterly* 9, no. 1 (1979): 17-21. Reprinted with permission.

doom for the white man's South. Thus when Lincoln won the election of 1860, the seven states of the Deep South—with their heavy slave concentrations—seceded from the Union and established a southern Confederacy dedicated to the preservation of Negro slavery. . . .

At the outset of the War, Lincoln strove to be consistent with all he and his party had said about slavery. His purpose in the struggle was to save the Union—and with it America's cherished experiment in popular government. He would crush the rebellion with his armies and restore the national authority in the rebel South with slavery intact. Then Lincoln and his party would resume and implement their policy of slave containment.

There were other reasons for Lincoln's hands-off policy about slavery. Since in 1861 he hoped for a speedy end to hostilities, he did not think emancipation a military necessity. In addition, four slave states—Delaware, Maryland, Kentucky, and Missouri—remained in the Union. Should he try to free the slaves, Lincoln feared it would send the crucial border spiraling into the Confederacy, something that would be catastrophic for the Union. He was also waging a bipartisan war effort, with northern Democrats and Republicans alike enlisting in his armies to save the Union. Lincoln encouraged this because he insisted that it would take a united North to win the War. An emancipation policy, he feared, would alienate northern Democrats, ignite a racial powderkeg in the loyal states (for he understood the anti-negro prejudice of most northern whites), and possibly cause a civil war in the rear. Then the Union really would be lost.

But the problems and pressures of Civil War caused Lincoln to change his mind, caused him to abandon his hands-off policy and hurl an executive fist at slavery in the rebel states, thus making emancipation a Union war objective. . . .

As the War ground on with no end in sight, he began wavering in his hands-off policy about slavery, began searching about for some compromise—something short of a sweeping emancipation decree. Still, he seemed caught in an impossible dilemma: how to remove the cause of the War, keep Britain out of the conflict, cripple the Confederacy and suppress this terrible rebellion, and yet retain the allegiance of northern Democrats and the critical border?

In March, 1862, he proposed a plan to Congress he thought might work: a gradual, compensated emancipation program to commence in the loyal border states. According to Lincoln's plan, the border states would abolish bondage voluntarily over the next thirty years, and the federal government would compensate slaveowners for their loss. At the same time, the national government would sponsor a colonization program, which was also to be entirely voluntary. Without a promise of colonization, Lincoln understood only too well, most northern whites would never accept emancipation, for fear that it would result in a mass exodus of southern Negroes into northern neighborhoods. For the rest of the year, every time he contemplated some new antislavery move, he made a great fuss about colonization: he embarked on a colonization project in central America and another in Haiti, and he held an interview about colonization with Washington Negroes, an interview he published in the press. In part, the ritual of colonization was designed to calm white racial fears in the North.

If his gradual, voluntary, state-guided plan were adopted, Lincoln contended that a presidential decree—federally enforced emancipation—would never be necessary. Abolition would begin on the local level in the loyal border and then be extended into the rebel states as they were conquered. Thus by a slow and salubrious process would the cause of the rebellion be removed and the future of a free union guaranteed.

The plan failed. It failed because the border states refused to act. In desperation, Lincoln on three different occasions—in the spring and summer of 1862—pleaded with border-state Congressmen to endorse his program. But most of them turned him down. They thought his plan would cost too much, would only whip the flames of rebellion, would sow dangerous discontent in their own states. Their intransigence was a sober lesson to Lincoln. It was proof indeed that slaveowners—even loyal slaveowners—were too tied up in the slave system ever to free their own Negroes and voluntarily transform their way of life. If abolition must come, it must begin in the rebel South by military action and then be extended into the loyal border later on. Which meant that the President must eradicate slavery himself. He could no longer avoid the responsibility. By mid-July, 1862, the pressures of what seemed an endless War had forced Lincoln to abandon his hands-off policy and lay a "strong hand on the colored element.". . .

On July 22, 1862, Lincoln summoned his Cabinet members and read them a draft of a Preliminary Emancipation Proclamation. Come January 1, 1863, in his capacity as Commander-in-Chief of the armed forces in time of war, Lincoln would free all the slaves in the rebel states. He would thus make it a Union objective to obliterate slavery as an institution in the Confederate South.

Contrary to what many historians have said, Lincoln's projected Proclamation went farther than anything Congress had done. True, Congress had just passed (and Lincoln had just signed) the Second Confiscation Act, which provided for the seizure and liberation of all slaves of people who supported or participated in the rebellion. Still, most slaves would be freed only after protracted case-by-case litigation in the federal courts. Another section of the act did liberate certain categories of slaves without court action, but the measure exempted loyal slaveowners in the rebel South, allowing them to keep their slaves and other property. Lincoln's Proclamation, on the other hand, was a sweeping blow against bondage as an institution in the rebel states, a blow that would free *all* the slaves there—those of loyalists and secessionists alike. Thus the President would handle emancipation himself, avoid judicial redtape, and use the military to vanquish the cornerstone of the Confederacy. Again, he justified this as a military necessity to save the Union—the world's last, best hope for popular government.

But William H. Seward and other Cabinet Secretaries dissuaded Lincoln from issuing his Proclamation in July. Seward argued that the Union had won no clear military victories, particularly in the showcase eastern theater. As a consequence, Europe would misconstrue the Proclamation as "our last shriek on the retreat," as a wild and reckless attempt to compensate for Union military ineptitude by provoking a slave insurrection behind the lines. So it was that Lincoln had to wait until the Army of the Potomac outfought Robert E. Lee's army at Antietam Creek in September, 1862, and Lee withdrew from the battlefield. Thereupon Lincoln issued his Preliminary Proclamation, with its warning that if the rebellion did not cease by January 1, 1863, the Executive branch would employ the Army and Navy to destroy bondage in the rebel states.

As it turned out, the Preliminary Proclamation ignited a powderbox of racial discontent in much of the lower North, especially the Midwest, and led to a Republican disaster in the fall by-elections of 1862. Already northern Democrats were unhappy with Lincoln's harsh war measures, especially his use of martial law and military arrests. But Negro emancipation was more than they could bear, and they stumped the northern states that fall, beating the drums of Negrophobia, warning of huge influxes of southern blacks into the North once emancipation came. Sullen, war weary, and racially aroused, northern voters dealt the Republicans a smashing blow, as the North's five most populous states—all of which had gone for Lincoln in 1860—now returned Democratic majorities to Congress. Republican analysts—and Lincoln himself—conceded that the Preliminary Proclamation was a major factor in the Republican defeat. But Lincoln told a delegation from Kentucky that he would rather die than retract a single word in his Proclamation.

As the New Year approached, conservative Republicans begged Lincoln to abandon his "reckless" emancipation scheme lest he shatter their demoralized party and wreck what remained of their country. But Lincoln stood firm. On New Year's day, 1863, he officially signed the final Emancipation Proclamation in the White House. His hand trembled badly, not because he was nervous, but because he had shaken hands all morning in a White House reception. He assured everyone present that he was never more certain of what he was doing. "If my name ever goes into history," he said, "it will be for this act." Then slowly and deliberately he wrote out his full name.

In the final Proclamation, Lincoln temporarily exempted occupied Tennessee and certain occupied places in Louisiana and Virginia. But later, in reconstructing those states, he withdrew the exemptions and made emancipation a mandatory part of his reconstruction program. He also excluded the loyal slave states because they were not in rebellion and he lacked the legal authority to remove slavery there. He would, however, keep pressing them to abolish bondage themselves—and would later push a constitutional amendment that liberated their slaves as well. With the exception of the loyal border and the designated occupied areas, the final Proclamation declared that as of this day, all slaves in the rebellious states were "forever free." Until the details of permanent legal freedom could be worked out, Lincoln ordered his armies to guarantee and protect the liberty of emancipated blacks. Finally, the Proclamation asserted that black men—southern and northern alike—would now be enlisted in Union military forces.

Lincoln's Proclamation was the most revolutionary measure ever to come from an American president thus far. As Union armies slashed into Confederate territory, they would uproot slavery as a state institution, automatically freeing all slaves in the areas and states they conquered. In this respect (as Lincoln said), the War brought on changes more fundamental and profound than either side had expected when the conflict began. Now slavery would perish as the Confederacy perished, would die by degrees with every Union advance, every Union victory.

Questions for Discussion

1. What were Lincoln's views on slavery and black people at the outset of the Civil War? When he issued the Emancipation Proclamation? Was he an abolitionist? A white supremacist?

2. Does Lincoln's decision to free the slaves mean that slavery was the main cause of the Civil War? What factors were most important to his decision-making process?

3. Do Lincoln's complex views diminish the worthiness of his actions? Are complicated heroes less heroic?

7

Reconstruction

Why Did Black Men Get the Vote Before Women?

In the aftermath of the Civil War, the nation was faced with the challenge of making itself whole again. It was clear that the rights of black Americans would be expanded during the period of Reconstruction, but just how expanded, and who else might be included in the growing sphere of American liberty, were the subject of fierce debate. The question of black male suffrage advanced by the Fifteenth Amendment was particularly divisive, setting erstwhile allies against one another as abolitionists and woman suffragists split over whether to support giving black men the vote before women of any color.

The Fourteenth Amendment, ratified in 1868, guaranteed a number of rights to black Americans but was elusive on the matter of granting black men the vote. The issue needed clarification, especially because several Southern states continued to withhold suffrage from the black race. If black men were to have a clear right to the ballot, another amendment was needed. To that end, the Republican Congress passed the Fifteenth Amendment, submitting it in 1869 to the states for ratification. In its entirety, the primary section of the Fifteenth Amendment reads:

> The right of citizens of the United States to vote shall not be denied or abridged by the United States or by any State on account of race, color, or previous condition of servitude.

These thirty-four words—or, more precisely, the lack of one word—split the suffrage movement into two camps. For several decades, abolitionists and woman suffragists had worked together in the common purpose of expanding rights to the unenfranchised segments of the population. The Fifteenth Amendment put that goal within reach for one group but excluded the other.

Some prominent suffragists like Elizabeth Cady Stanton and Susan B. Anthony refused to support the Fifteenth Amendment unless discrimination on the basis of sex was also prohibited. They formed the National Woman Suffrage Association to advocate the enfranchisement of "Saxon" (read: white) women before black men, and in speeches and articles in their women's rights newspaper, *The Revolution*, their anger often veered into racism. Elizabeth Cady Stanton, an abolitionist with ties to the Underground Railroad prior to the war, complained of giving black "Sambo" the vote before white ladies of standing. Other longtime supporters of woman suffrage, including leading abolitionists like the former slave Frederick Douglass, the philanthropist and reformer Gerrit Smith (who was also Stanton's cousin), the suffragist Lucy Stone, and the Radical Republican leaders Wendell Phillips and Thaddeus Stevens, decided that the urgent need of black men to protect themselves against continuing Southern persecution demanded passage of the amendment. Lucy Stone and other supporters of the measure formed the American Woman Suffrage Association.

Many abolitionists continued to work determinedly for woman suffrage after the Fifteenth Amendment was ratified in 1870. But it was to be two more decades before the factions of the suffrage movement formally reunited as the National American Woman Suffrage Association. Together they would work for thirty more years to see the passage of the Nineteenth Amendment in 1920, finally guaranteeing women the right to vote and making suffrage universal among the nation's citizens.

Gerrit Smith on Petitions
Elizabeth Cady Stanton

Peterboro, December 30, 1868

My Dear Susan B. Anthony: I this evening receive your earnest letter. It pains me to be obliged to disappoint you. But I cannot sign the Petition you send me. Cheerfully, gladly can I sign a Petition for the enfranchisement of

From Elizabeth Cady Stanton, "Gerrit Smith on Petitions," *The Revolution* (January 14, 1869): 24-5.

women. But I cannot sign a paper against the enfranchisement of the negro man, unless at the same time woman
shall be enfranchised. The removal of the political disabili-
ties of race is my first desire, of sex, my second. If put on
the same level and urged in the same connection neither
will be soon accomplished. The former will very soon be, if
untrammelled by the other, and its success will prepare the
way for the accomplishment of the other.

With great regard your friend,
GERRIT SMITH.

To the Senate and House of Representatives, in Congress
Assembled:

The undersigned, citizens of the State of _____ earnestly
but respectfully request that, in any change or amendment
of the Constitution you may propose to extend or regulate
Suffrage, there shall be no distinctions made between men
and women.

The above is the petition to which our friend Gerrit Smith, as an
abolitionist, cannot conscientiously put his name, while republicans
and democrats are signing it all over the country. He does not clearly
read the signs of the times, or he would see that there is to be no reconstruction of this nation, except on the basis of Universal Suffrage,
as the natural, inalienable right of every citizen to its exercise is the
only logical ground on which to base an argument. The uprising of
the women on both continents, in France, England, Russia, Switzer-
land, and the United States all show that advancing civilization demands a new element in the government of nations.

As the aristocracy in this country is the "male sex," and as Mr.
Smith belongs to the privileged order, he naturally considers it important, for the best interests of the nation, that every type and shade
of degraded, ignorant manhood should be enfranchised, before even
the higher classes of womanhood should be admitted to the polls.

This does not surprise us! Men always judge more wisely of objective wrongs and oppressions, than of those in which they are themselves involved. Tyranny on a southern plantation is far more easily
seen by white men at the north than the wrongs of the women of
their own households. . . .

[I]n criticising such good and noble men as Gerrit Smith and Wendell Phillips for their apathy on Woman's enfranchisement at this hour,
it is not because we think their course at all remarkable, nor that we

have the least hope of influencing *them,* but simply to rouse the women of the country to the fact that they must not look to these men for their champions at this hour. But what does surprise us in this cry of "manhood suffrage" is that every *woman* does not see in it national suicide, and her own destruction. In view of the present demoralization of our government, bribery and corruption alike in the legislative, the executive and judicial branches, drunkenness in the White House, Congress, and every state legislature . . . what thinking mind can look for any improvement, in extending suffrage still further to the very class that have produced this state of things.

While philosophy and science alike point to woman, as the new power destined to redeem the world, how can Mr. Smith fail to see that it is just this we need to restore honor and virtue in government? When society in California and Oregon was chiefly male and rapidly tending to savageism [*sic*], ship loads of women went out, and restored order and decency to life. Would black men have availed anything among those white savages? There is sex in the spiritual as well as the physical, and what we need to-day in government, in the world of morals and thought, is the recognition of the feminine element, as it is this alone that can hold the masculine in check.

Again: Mr. Smith refuses to sign the petition, because he thinks to press the broader question of "Universal Suffrage" would defeat the partial one of "Manhood Suffrage"; in other words, to demand protection for women against her oppressors, would jeopardize the black man's chance of securing protection against his oppressors. If it is a question of precedence merely, on what principle of justice or courtesy should woman yield her right of enfranchisement to the negro? If men cannot be trusted to legislate for their own sex, how can they legislate for the opposite sex, of whose wants and needs they know nothing! It has always been considered good philosophy in pressing any measure to claim the uttermost in order to get something. . . . Henry Ward Beecher advised abolitionists, right after the war, to demand "Universal Suffrage" if they wished to secure the ballot for the new made freedmen. "Bait your hooks," said he, "with a woman and perhaps you will catch a negro." But their intense interest in the negro blinded them, and they foresook principle for policy, and in giving woman the cold shoulder they raised a more deadly opposition to the negro than any we had yet encountered, creating an antagonism between him, and the very element most needed, especially at the south, to be propitiated in his behalf. It was this feeling that defeated "negro suffrage" in Kansas. . . .

[A]lthough that state always gives large republican majorities and "negro suffrage" was a party measure, politicians, party, press, were alike powerless before the deep settled indignation of the women at the proposition to place the negro above their own heads.

Such was their feeling in the matter that the mass of the men everywhere pledged that if the women were not enfranchised, neither should the negro be. The result was that the vote for woman's suffrage, without party, press or thorough canvass of the state, lacked of a few hundred of the vote of the great republican party for negro suffrage. Had republicans and abolitionists advocated both propositions, they would have been triumphantly carried. What is true in Kansas will prove equally true for every state in this Union; there can be no reconstruction of this government on any basis other than universal suffrage. There is no other ground on which to debate the question. Every argument for the negro is an argument for woman and no logician can escape it.

But Mr. Smith abandons the principle clearly involved, and entrenches himself on policy. He would undoubtedly plead the necessity of the ballot for the negro at the south for his protection, and points us to innumerable acts of cruelty he suffers to-day. But all these things fall as heavily on the women of the black race, yea far more so, for no man can ever know the deep, the damning degradation to which woman is subject in her youth, helplessness and poverty. The enfranchisement of the men of her race, Mr. Smith would say, is her protection.

Our Saxon men have held the ballot in this country for a century, and what honest man can claim that it has been used for woman's protection? Alas! we have given the very heyday of our life to undoing the cruel and unjust laws that the men of New York had made for their own mothers, wives and daughters. Have Saxon women no wrongs to right, and will they be better protected when negroes are their rulers? Remember that all woman needs protection against to-day is man, read the following:

SUPPOSED INFANTICIDE

A young girl named Abson, who has for the past few months been an inmate of the Hudson County poorhouse, at Snake Hill, gave birth, four days ago, to a child of negro parentage, which was found dead in a bed yesterday morning, supposed to have been smothered by its mother. . . . About a year ago, at which time she was fourteen years of age, the girl was sent to work on a farm at Rockaway [New Jersey]. During the absence of her employer's family, a negro on the farm effected her ruin, which, being discovered, and she being enciente, she was sent to . . . the Almshouse, where the child was born, and killed as stated. Coroner Warren will hold an inquest.

With judges and jurors of negroes, remembering the generations of wrong and injustice their daughters have suffered at the white man's hands, how will Saxon girls fare in their courts for crimes like this?

How do they fare in our own courts to-day, tried by Saxon fathers, husbands, brothers, sons? Hester Vaughn, a young English girl, under sentence of death for the alleged crime of Infanticide, which could not be proved against her, has dragged the weary days of a whole year away in the solitude and gloom of a Pennsylvania prison, while he who betrayed her walks this green earth in freedom. . . .

Such is "manhood suffrage." Shall we prolong and perpetuate injustice like this, and increase its power by adding more ignorance and brutality, and thus risk worse oppressions for ourselves and our daughters? Society, as organized to-day under the man power, is one grand rape of womanhood, on the highways, in our jails, prisons, asylums, in our homes, alike in the world of fashion and of work. Hence, discord, despair, violence, crime, the blind, the deaf, the dumb, the idiot, the lunatic, the drunkard, all that was inverted and must be so, until the mother of the race be made dictator in the social realm. To this end we need every power to lift her up, and teach mankind that in all God's universe there is nothing so holy and sacred as womanhood. Do such men as Gerrit Smith and Wendell Phillips teach this lesson to the lower order of men who learn truth and justice from their lips, when they tell the most noble, virtuous, educated matrons of this republic, to stand back, until all the sons of Adam are clothed with citizenship? Do they teach woman self-respect when they tell her to hold her claims to virtue, honor and dignity in abeyance to those of *manhood*? . . .

Although those who demand "Woman's Suffrage" on principle are few, those who would oppose "Negro Suffrage" from prejudice are many; hence the only way to secure the latter is to end all this talk of class legislation, bury the negro in the citizen, and claim the suffrage for all men and women, as a natural, inalienable right. The friends of the negro never made a greater blunder, than when, at the close of the war, they timidly refused to lead the nation, in demanding suffrage for all. If even Wendell Phillips and Gerrit Smith, the very apostles of democracy upon this continent, failed at that point, how can we wonder at the vacillation and confusion of mere politicians at this hour? . . . We have pressed these considerations so often on Mr. Phillips and Mr. Smith, during the last four years, that we fear we have entirely forfeited the friendship of the one, and diminished the confidence of the other in our good judgment; but time, that rights all wrongs, will surely bring them back to the standpoint of principle.

An Urgency to Obtain the Ballot
Frederick Douglass

TO JOSEPHINE SOPHIE WHITE GRIFFING

Rochester [New York], Sept. 27, 1868

My dear Friend:

I am impelled by no lack of generosity in refusing to come to Washington to speak in behalf of woman's suffrage. The right of woman to vote is as sacred in my judgment as that of man, and I am quite willing at any time to hold up both hands in favor of this right. It does not however follow that I can come to Washington or go elsewhere to deliver lectures upon this special subject. I am now devoting myself to a cause not more sacred, certainly more urgent, because it is one of life and death to the long-enslaved people of this country, and this is: negro suffrage. While the negro is mobbed, beaten, shot, stabbed, hanged, burnt and is the target of all that is malignant in the North and all that is murderous in the South, his claims may be preferred by me without exposing in any wise myself to the imputation of narrowness or meanness toward the cause of woman. As you very well know, woman has a thousand ways to attach herself to the governing power of the land and already exerts an honorable influence on the course of legislation. She is the victim of abuses, to be sure, but it cannot be pretended I think that her cause is as urgent as that of ours. I never suspected you of sympathizing with Miss Anthony and Mrs. Stanton in their course. Their principle is: that no negro shall be enfranchised while woman is not. Now, considering that white men have been enfranchised always, and colored men have not, the conduct of these white women, whose husbands, fathers and brothers are voters, does not seem generous.

> Very truly yours-
> Fredk Douglass

From Frederick Douglass, "To Josephine Sophie White Griffing, Rochester, Sept. 27, 1868"; "Proceedings of the American Equal Rights Association Convention, Steinway Hall, New York City, May 12, 1869," in Elizabeth Cady Stanton, Susan B. Anthony, and Matilda Joslyn Gage, eds. *History of Woman Suffrage* (New York: Fowler & Wells, 1882), 382-4.

AT THE AMERICAN EQUAL RIGHTS
ASSOCIATION CONVENTION

New York City, May 12, 1869

Mr. DOUGLASS:—I came here more as a listener than to speak, and I have listened with a great deal of pleasure. . . . There is no name greater than that of Elizabeth Cady Stanton in the matter of woman's rights and equal rights, but my sentiments are tinged a little against *The Revolution*. There was in the address to which I allude the employment of certain names, such as "Sambo," and the gardener, and the bootblack, and the daughters of Jefferson and Washington, and all the rest that I can not coincide with. I have asked what difference there is between the daughters of Jefferson and Washington and other daughters. (Laughter.) I must say that I do not see how any one can pretend that there is the same urgency in giving the ballot to woman as to the negro. With us, the matter is a question of life and death, at least, in fifteen States of the Union. When women, because they are women, are hunted down through the cities of New York and New Orleans; when they are dragged from their houses and hung upon lamp-posts; when their children are torn from their arms, and their brains dashed out upon the pavement; when they are objects of insult and outrage at every turn; when they are in danger of having their homes burnt down over their heads; when their children are not allowed to enter schools; then they will have an urgency to obtain the ballot equal to our own. (Great applause.)

A VOICE:—Is that not all true about black women?

Mr. DOUGLASS:—Yes, yes, yes; it is true of the black woman, but not because she is a woman, but because she is black. (Applause.) Julia Ward Howe at the conclusion of her great speech delivered at the convention in Boston last year, said: "I am willing that the negro shall get the ballot before me." (Applause.) Woman! why, she has 10,000 modes of grappling with her difficulties. I believe that all the virtue of the world can take care of all the evil. I believe that all the intelligence can take care of all the ignorance. (Applause.) I am in favor of woman's suffrage in order that we shall have all the virtue and vice confronted. Let me tell you that when there were few houses in which the black man could have put his head, this woolly head of mine found a refuge in the house of Mrs. Elizabeth Cady Stanton, and if I had been blacker than sixteen midnights, without a single star, it would have been the same. (Applause.)

Miss ANTHONY:—The old anti-slavery school say women must stand back and wait until the negroes shall be recognized. But we say, if you will not give the whole loaf of suffrage to the entire people, give it to the most intelligent first. (Applause.) If intelligence, justice, and morality are to have precedence in the Government, let the question of woman be brought up first and that of the negro last. (Applause.) While I was canvassing the State with petitions and had them filled with names for our cause to the Legislature, a man dared to say to me that the freedom of women was all a theory and not a practical thing. (Applause.) When Mr. Douglass mentioned the black man first and the woman last, if he had noticed he would have seen that it was the men that clapped and not the women. There is not the woman born who desires to eat the bread of dependence, no matter whether it be from the hand of father, husband, or brother; for any one who does so eat her bread places herself in the power of the person from whom she takes it. (Applause.) Mr. Douglass talks about the wrongs of the negro; but with all the outrages that he to-day suffers, he would not exchange his sex and take the place of Elizabeth Cady Stanton. (Laughter and applause.)

Mr. DOUGLASS:—I want to know if granting you the right of suffrage will change the nature of our sexes? (Great laughter.)

Miss ANTHONY:—It will change the pecuniary position of woman; it will place her where she can earn her own bread. (Loud applause.) She will not then be driven to such employments only as man chooses for her. . . .

Mrs. LUCY STONE:—Mrs. Stanton will, of course, advocate the precedence for her sex, and Mr. Douglass will strive for the first position for his, and both are perhaps right. If it be true that the government derives its authority from the consent of the governed, we are safe in trusting that principle to the uttermost. If one has a right to say that you can not read and therefore can not vote, then it may be said that you are a woman and therefore can not vote. We are lost if we turn away from the middle principle and argue for one class. I was once a teacher among fugitive slaves. There was one old man, and every tooth was gone, his hair was white, and his face was full of wrinkles, yet, day after day and hour after hour, he came up to the school-house and tried with patience to learn to read, and by-and-by, when he had spelled out the first few verses of the first chapter of the Gospel of St. John, he said to me, "Now, I want to learn to write." I tried to make him satisfied with what he had acquired, but the old man said, "Mrs. Stone, somewhere in the wide world I have a son; I have not heard from him in twenty years; if I should hear from him, I want to write to him, so take hold of my hand and teach me." I did, but before he had proceeded in many lessons, the angels came and gathered him up and bore him to his Father. Let no man speak of an educated suffrage. The gentleman who addressed you claimed that the negroes had the first right to the suffrage, and drew a picture which only his great word-power can do. He again in Massachusetts, when it had cast a majority in favor of Grant and negro suffrage, stood upon the platform and said that woman had better wait for the negro; that is, that both could not be carried, and that the negro had better be the one. But I freely forgave him because he felt as he spoke. But woman suffrage is more imperative than his own; and I want to remind the audience that when he says what the Ku-Kluxes did all over the South, the Ku-Kluxes here in the North in the shape of men, take away the children from the mother, and separate them as completely as if done on the block of the auctioneer. Over in New Jersey they have a law which says that *any* father—he might be the most brutal man that ever existed—*any* father, it says, whether he be under age or not, may by his last will and testament dispose of the custody of his child, born or to be born, and that such disposition shall be good against all persons, and that the mother may not recover her child; and that law modified in form exists over every State in the Union except in Kansas. Woman has an ocean of wrongs too deep for any plummet, and the negro, too, has an ocean of wrongs that can not be fathomed. There are two great oceans; in the one is the black man, and in the other is the woman. But I thank God for that XV. Amendment, and hope that it will be adopted in every State. I will be thankful in my soul if *any* body can get out of the terrible pit. But I believe that the safety of the government would be more promoted by the admission of woman as an element of restoration and harmony than the negro. I believe that the influence of woman will save the country before every other power. (Applause.) I see the signs of the times pointing to this consummation, and I believe that in some parts of the country women will vote for the President of these United States in 1872. (Applause.)

Questions for Discussion

1. Among the arguments presented by defenders and opponents of the Fifteenth Amendment, which do you find most compelling?

2. Was Reconstruction an appropriate time to push for woman suffrage in addition to that of black manhood? Do you think it possible that the argument some women suffragists made against the Fifteenth Amendment ultimately delayed the adoption of the Nineteenth Amendment, which gave to all female citizens the right to vote that some states and territories had already granted them?

3. Although black men got the right to vote in 1870, many were effectively barred from the polls in the South by Jim Crow laws until the 1960s. Do you think this would have been the case if the Fifteenth Amendment had also enfranchised women?

4. In the American democratic system, is it politically effective to cling to absolute principles like universal suffrage or abolition? What are the advantages and disadvantages of refusing to compromise an important ideal?

8

Westward Expansion

Were Christian Missionaries to the Western Indian Tribes Agents of Imperialism?

On the morning of December 29, 1890, Chief Big Foot's band of Lakota Sioux—350 men, women and children, including a few survivors of Sitting Bull's shattered band—assembled near the banks of Wounded Knee Creek, on the Pine Ridge Reservation in South Dakota, to surrender to the Seventh Cavalry of the United States Army. Something went wrong (exactly what is still disputed), and the fighting that ensued, alternately called a battle and a massacre, has often since been marked by historians as the end of the Indian Wars, the place where indigenous resistance was finally broken in the name of Manifest Destiny.

In many ways, the defeat of the Lakota at Wounded Knee was the culmination of the policy of Indian Removal begun during the presidency of Andrew Jackson, which was itself the codification of a line of Indian policy that EuroAmerican settlers had pursued since early colonial days. Between the early seventeenth century and the end of the nineteenth, British colonists and then white Americans repeatedly used diplomacy, coercion, and violence—often a combination of all three—to move tribes off of land desired for white settlement. Yet there was more to the nation's westward expansion than forced removal and military might: Christian missionaries, sent and supported by denominations based in the East, persistently pushed out into areas still under tribal control to bring their faith to the Indians.

Devout men and women, many inspired by the revivalism of the

Second Great Awakening, set out to convert Indians, whom they regarded as heathens lost to heaven unless they accepted the Biblical message. While some of these missionaries may have had no ulterior motive beyond bringing salvation to lost souls, others saw themselves in the dual role of apostle to the unsaved and advanced guard of white civilization. These missionaries did not see the two efforts as contradictory, and their pride in helping the nation realize its Manifest Destiny does not impugn the sincerity of their desire to help the Indians. But whatever the intentions of the missionaries, the Indians (most of whom tolerated the missionaries, at least initially) noticed that their arrival often presaged an increased white presence in the area.

In some cases, as in the story of Narcissa Whitman told by the historian Patricia Nelson Limerick, the Indians turned violently against the missionaries. Yet Professor Limerick hesitates to label the missionary either victim or villain; the complexity of her story defies such simple categories. A leading voice among a group of scholars known as New Western Historians, Limerick does not hesitate to describe EuroAmerican westward expansion as conquest, but her examination of the complex motives and convictions of people who converged in the West resists simplification into clear-cut heroes or scoundrels. For her, the legacy of this conquest is multifaceted and continues to be felt throughout the modern West. George E. Tinker, of Osage and Cherokee ancestry and a professor of Indian culture and religion, agrees with much of Limerick's characterization of Western history, especially the continuity of past and present, but contends that the work of the missionaries amounted to cultural genocide against the tribes. Although he does not claim that the Christian missionaries set out to destroy the Indians—quite the contrary, in fact—Tinker argues that the result of their actions cannot be explained away as an unfortunate unforeseen consequence. He is much more willing to paint the missionaries as villains: "At some level," he concludes, "they must have known what they were about."

The Legacy of Conquest
Patricia Nelson Limerick

Narcissa Prentiss Whitman made a very unlikely villain. Deeply moved by the thought of Western Indians living without knowledge of Christianity, Narcissa Prentiss wrote her mission board in 1835, "I

From Patricia Nelson Limerick, *The Legacy of Conquest: The Unbroken Past of the American West* (New York: W.W. Norton, 1987), 37-41. Reprinted with permission.

now offer myself to the American Board to be employed in their service among the heathen. . . ." In 1836, she left her home in New York to rescue the Indians in Oregon. An unattached female could hardly be a missionary, and before her departure Narcissa Prentiss hastily married another Oregon volunteer, Marcus Whitman. The Whitmans and Henry and Eliza Spalding set off to cross the country. Pioneers on the overland trail, they faced stiff challenges from nature and some from human nature. The fur trappers and traders with whom they traveled resented the delays and sermons that came with missionary companionship. The missionaries themselves presented less than a united front. They had the strong, contentious personalities of self-appointed agents of God. They also had a history; Henry Spalding had courted Narcissa, and lost. Anyone who thinks of the nineteenth-century West as a land of fresh starts and new beginnings might think of Henry Spalding and Narcissa Whitman and the memories they took with them to Oregon.

Arrived in the Oregon country, the missionaries—like salesmen dividing up markets—divided up tribes and locations. The Whitmans set to work on the Cayuse Indians. Narcissa Whitman's life in Oregon provides little support for the image of life in the West as free, adventurous, and romantic. Most of the time, she labored. She had one child of her own; she adopted many others—mixed-blood children of fur trappers, and orphans from the overland trail. "My health has been so poor," she wrote her sister in 1846, "and my family has increased so rapidly, that it has been impossible. You will be astonished to know that we have eleven children in our family, and not one of them our own by birth, but so it is. Seven orphans were brought to our door in Oct., 1844, whose parents both died on the way to this country. Destitute and friendless, there was no other alternative—we must take them in or they must perish."

Depending on one's point of view, the Whitman mission had a lucky or an unlucky location—along the Oregon Trail, where exhausted travelers arrived desperate for food, rest, and help. Narcissa Whitman's small home served as kitchen, dining hall, dormitory, and church building, while she longed for privacy and rest. She often cooked three meals a day for twenty people. For five years, she had no stove and cooked in an open fireplace.

In the midst of crowds, she was lonely, writing nostalgic letters to friends and family in the East who seemed to answer infrequently; she went as long as two years without a letter from home. Separated by distance and sometimes by quarrels, Narcissa and the other missionary wives in Oregon tried for a time to organize a nineteenth-century version of a woman's support group; at a certain hour every day, they would pause in their work, think of each other, and pray for the strength to be proper mothers to their children in the wilderness.

Direct tragedy added to loneliness, overwork, and frustration. The Whitmans' only child, two years old, drowned while playing alone near a stream. Providence was testing Narcissa Whitman's faith in every imaginable way.

Then, in November of 1847, after eleven years with the missionaries among them, when the white or mixed-blood mission population had grown to twenty men, ten women, and forty-four children, the Cayuse Indians rose in rebellion and killed fourteen people—including Marcus and Narcissa Whitman.

Was Narcissa Whitman an innocent victim of brutality and ingratitude? What possessed the Cayuses?

One skill essential to the writing of Western American history is a capacity to deal with multiple points of view. It is as if one were a lawyer at a trial designed on the principle of the Mad Hatter's tea party—as soon as one begins to understand and empathize with the plaintiff's case, it is time to move over and empathize with the defendant. Seldom are there only two parties or only two points of view. Taking into account division within groups—intertribal conflict and factions within tribes and, in Oregon, settlers against missionaries, Protestants against Catholics, British Hudson's Bay Company traders against Americans—it is taxing simply to keep track of the points of view.

Why did the Cayuses kill the Whitmans? The chain of events bringing the Whitmans to the Northwest was an odd and arbitrary one. In a recent book, the historian Christopher Miller explains that the Whitman mission was hardly the first crisis to hit the Columbia Plateau and its natives. A "three hundred year cold spell," a "result of the Little Ice Age," had shaken the environment, apparently reducing food sources. Moreover, the effects of European presence in North America began reaching the plateau even before the Europeans themselves arrived. The "conjunction of sickness, with the coming of horses, guns, climatic deterioration and near constant war" added up to an "eighteenth-century crisis." Punctuated by a disturbing and perplexing ash fall from a volcanic explosion, the changes brought many of the Plateau Indians to the conviction that the world was in trouble. They were thus receptive to a new set of prophecies from religious leaders. A central element of this new worldview came in the reported words of the man known as the Spokan Prophet, words spoken around 1790: "Soon there will come from the rising sun a different kind of man from any you have yet seen, who will bring with them a book and will teach you everything, after that the world will fall to pieces," opening the way to a restored and better world. Groups of Indians therefore began to welcome whites, since learning from these newcomers was to be an essential stage in the route to a new future.

In 1831, a small party of Nez Perce and Flathead Indians journeyed to St. Louis, Missouri. For years, Western historians said that these Indians had heard of Jesuits through contacts with fur traders and had come to ask for their own "Black Robes." That confident claim aside, Christopher Miller has recently written that it is still a "mystery how it all came to pass." Nonetheless, he argues persuasively that the Northwest Indians went to St. Louis pursuing religious fulfillment according to the plateau millennial tradition; it was their unlikely fate to be misunderstood by the equally millennial Christians who heard the story of the visit. A Protestant man named William Walker wrote a letter about the meetings in St. Louis, and the letter was circulated in church newspapers and read at church meetings, leaving the impression that the Indians of Oregon were begging for Christianity.

And so, in this chain of circumstances "so bizarre as to seem providential," in Miller's words, the Cayuses got the Whitmans, who had responded to the furor provoked by the letter. Irritations began to pile up. The Whitmans set out to transform the Cayuses from hunters, fishers, and gatherers to farmers, from heathens to Presbyterians. As the place became a way station for the Oregon Trail, the mission began to look like an agency for the service of white people. This was not, in fact, too far from the founder's view of his organization. "It does not concern me so much what is to become of any particular set of Indians," Marcus Whitman wrote his parents, "as to give them the offer of salvation through the gospel and the opportunity of civilization. . . . I have no doubt our greatest work is to be to aid the white settlement of this country and help to found its religious institutions." The Cayuses began to suffer from white people's diseases, to which they had no immunity. Finally, in 1847, they were devastated by measles. While the white people at the mission seldom died from measles, the Indians noticed that an infected Cayuse nearly always died. It was an Indian conviction that disease was "the result of either malevolence or spiritual transgression"; either way, the evidence pointed at the missionaries. When the Cayuses finally turned on the Whitmans, they were giving up "the shared prophetic vision" that these newcomers would teach a lesson essential to reshaping the world. The Cayuses were, in other words, acting in and responding to currents of history of which Narcissa Whitman was not a primary determinant.

Descending on the Cayuses, determined to bring light to the "benighted ones" living in "the thick darkness of heathenism," Narcissa Whitman was an intolerant invader. If she was not a villain, neither was she an innocent victim. Her story is melancholy but on the whole predictable, one of many similar stories in Western history that trigger an interventionist's urge. "Watch out, Narcissa," one finds oneself thinking, 140 years too late, "you think you are doing good works, but you are getting yourself—and others—into deep trouble." Given the inability of Cayuses to understand Presbyterians, and the inability of Presbyterians to understand Cayuses, the trouble could only escalate. Narcissa Whitman would not have imagined that there was anything to understand; where the Cayuses had religion, social networks, a thriving trade in horses, and a full culture, Whitman would have seen vacancy or, worse, heathenism.

Narcissa Whitman knew she was volunteering for risk; her willingness to take on those risks is, however, easier to understand because it was based on religion. Irrational faith is its own explanation; one can analyze its components, but the fact remains that extraordinary faith leads to extraordinary action. The mystery is not that Narcissa Whitman risked all for the demands of the deity but that so many others risked [the hardships and hazards of going West] for the demands of the profit motive.

Missionary Conquest
George E. Tinker

The motivation and the theoretical basis for the missionary endeavor, apparent both from the actual practice of the missionaries and from their writings, will demonstrate that they not only preached a new gospel of salvation, but also just as energetically imposed a new cultural model for existence on Indian people. The evidence will show that these two tasks became nearly indistinguishable in practice.

To state the case baldly and dramatically, my thesis is that the Christian missionaries—of all denominations working among American Indian nations—were partners in genocide. Unwittingly no doubt, and always with the best of intentions, nevertheless the missionaries were guilty of complicity in the destruction of Indian cultures and tribal social structures—complicity in the devastating impoverishment and death of the people to whom they preached. I will explore the extent to which each of these missionary heroes implicitly blurred any distinction between the gospel of salvation and their own culture. This blurring invariably resulted in the missionary's culture, values, and social and political structures, not to say political hegemony and control, being imposed on tribal peoples, all in the name of the gospel. . . .

I must stress that my point is not simply to criticize these departed

From George E. Tinker, *Missionary Conquest: The Gospel and Native American Cultural Genocide* (Minneapolis: Fortress Press, 1993), 4-6, 15-8. Reprinted with permission.

heroes nor to punish their memory; nor do I wish to impose a burden of guilt on their existing denominations or heirs today. Rather, I intend to expose the illusion, the covert "lie" of white self-righteousness as it was internalized and acted out by the missionaries themselves. I do this out of a sense that this is part of America's unfinished business. Tangentially, it becomes a contribution to our understanding of why Native American peoples have generally failed to enter the American mainstream and continue to live in poverty and oppression, marginalized on the periphery of society. By and large, Indian people have not found liberation in the gospel of Jesus Christ, but, rather, continued bondage to a culture that is both alien and alienating, and even genocidal against American Indian peoples. . . .

To accuse . . . any of these missionaries of genocide will require some preliminary discussion of the concept at stake. Most importantly, it will require a broader definition of genocide than is generally used. In addition to the straightforward executions of military conquest or police action, such a broader definition must include the notion of cultural genocide and the interrelated subcategories of political, economic, social, and religious genocide. When people are killed as a military tactic or as part of a police action, intended to systematically exterminate a people in the service of some political end, genocide's violence and bloodshed are readily apparent, especially when a policy of genocide is clearly articulated by the perpetrating political entity, as it was in Nazi Germany. That Native American peoples were also subjected to genocide should be self-evident, although it was rarely articulated as policy.

In 1948, in response to the systematic murder of Jews and others in Nazi Germany, the United Nations Genocide Convention began the process of broadening our understanding by defining genocide as "any of several kinds of acts committed with intent to destroy, in whole or in part, a national, ethnic, racial or religious group, as such." The definition proposed here moves beyond the United Nations definition in one critical respect. Namely, I am arguing that the conscious intent to destroy a people is not necessary for an act to be genocidal or for it to succeed in destroying. What I call cultural genocide functions at times as conscious intent, but at other times at such a systemic level that it may be largely subliminal. In such cases, the good intent of some may be so mired in unrecognized systemic structures that they even remain unaware of the destruction that results from those good intentions.

Cultural genocide is more subtle than overt military extermination, yet it is no less devastating to a people. Although the evidence is clear that [Spanish Franciscan priest Junípero] Serra's missionary empire [in California during the eighteenth century] engaged in severe corporal punishment, there is certainly no evidence that missionaries ever engaged in the systematic killing of Indian people (with the exception, of course, of "Col." John Chivington at Sand Creek [Colorado], who was a former missionary and the Methodist district superintendent in Denver when he volunteered for military service [that culminated in a massacre of peaceful Cheyenne Indians in 1864]). Nevertheless, the Native American population of coastal California was reduced by some 90 percent during seventy years under the sole proprietorship of Serra's mission system. Imported diseases, especially "virgin soil" epidemics, are usually cited as the cause for such devastating statistics. Yet the effects of the European invasion on the culture, political structure, and economics of the people call for a thorough analysis of all the effects of the missions in California, including the extent to which the evangelizing effort weakened the native cultures so as to imperil the very survival of the people.

Cultural genocide can be defined as the effective destruction of a people by systematically or systemically (intentionally or unintentionally in order to achieve other goals) destroying, eroding, or undermining the integrity of the culture and system of values that defines a people and gives them life. First of all, it involves the destruction of those cultural structures of existence that give a people a sense of holistic and communal integrity. It does this by limiting a people's freedom to practice their culture and to live out their lives in culturally appropriate patterns. It effectively destroys a people by eroding both their self-esteem and the interrelationships that bind them together as a community. In North American mission history, cultural genocide almost always involved an attack on the spiritual foundations of a people's unity by denying the existing ceremonial and mythological sense of a community in relationship to the Sacred Other. Finally, it erodes a people's self-image as a whole people by attacking or belittling every aspect of native culture. . . .

At one level at least, I have presumed a certain naïveté with respect to the complicity of the missionaries in acts of cultural genocide. They surely did not intend any harm to Indian people, yet their blindness to their own inculturation of European values and social structures meant that complicity was unavoidable. That is, even at this initial level of analysis, it is clear that the missionaries were myopic regarding their own cultural biases. They engaged in actions that were a genuinely naive imposition of their own cultural values and models of society on tribal peoples for whom the experience became dislocative and disruptive. The goals of the missionaries emerged out of a reservoir of what [the philosopher] Wittgenstein called "common sense knowledge." They could reflect on that knowledge only within the limitations of their contemporary cultural self-awareness. The parameters of the world are defined by the subjective perception of the individual and the cultural community of individuals who tend to communicate easily with one another and agree generally about the interpretation of their experiences. The missionaries all came to Native American tribal communities with firmly established commitments to their own European or Euroamerican cultures with their social structures and institutions. As a result, they naturally assumed the superiority of the institutions and social structures of their own world and readily imposed them on Indian people. At the bottom line, then, this cultural myopia of the missionaries functioned to facilitate the exploitation of Indian people by both the government and the private sector or by the land-hungry immigrant farmers encroaching ever further onto the plains. Identifying their actions as well-intentioned but misguided certainly does not exonerate the missionaries. It merely serves to explain behavior that is finally inconsistent with the goal of salvation they proclaimed, and as responsible human beings they must be held accountable for the disastrous consequences of their actions.

At this level of analysis, the failure of the missionaries must be understood not just in individual terms but as systemic failure. The culpability of the individual missionaries for imposing their culture on Native Americans and perpetuating the lie of white superiority was in actuality prescribed from the outset by European and Euroamerican social structures. That is to say, it was impossible for any missionary to avoid complicity in the genocide of Native American peoples. Again in this case, recognizing the broader, structural impetus of Western social structures toward the assertion of white hegemony dare not become an excuse for exonerating the individual's participation in the dysfunctionality of the whole. . . .

Finally, at a certain level of analysis, the presumed naïveté of the missionaries begins to fade as a justification for their behavior, and it becomes far more difficult to protect their memory even minimally by appealing to the spirit of the times or the pervasiveness of attitudes among Euroamerican peoples. How could these dedicated spiritual figures not see the role they inevitably played in the economic exploitation or the political manipulation of the tribal peoples of North America? More devastating to Indian communities than the imposition of new cultural standards was the missionaries' tendency to act consistently, sometimes self-consciously and sometimes implicitly, in the best interests of the economic and political structures of their Western cultural world. Thus, it was almost natural for the missionaries to participate in the political process of subjugation and to support the repressive efforts of their own government in whatever program had been devised at the time to serve that interest. It was just as natural for them to support the economic enterprises that manipulated and exploited Indian labor and resources. What finally must be realized is that the missionaries were deeply involved in symbiotic relationships with the very structures of power that crushed Indian resistance to the European invasion every step of the way, as Manifest Destiny moved "From California to the New York Island, from the redwood forest to the gulf stream waters. . . ."

At some point we must conclude that good intentions did not simply fail but were suspect from the beginning. One could argue that naïveté dissolves when a mission institution accepts government monies . . . in order to pursue its missionary outreach. At that point the church receiving the funds made the decision to serve the interests of the U.S. government. Even if the church had completely confused its own proclamation of the gospel with the interests of the government, the relationship between government and church predicates that the missionaries' activity with regard to native peoples was no longer simply an act of cultural unconsciousness. . . . The impetus to power and authority, the impetus to rule, is not naïveté. A similar breakdown of good intentions can be demonstrated for virtually every important missionary in the history of Native American missions in both hemispheres.

One aspect of this missionary complicity must remain somewhat enigmatic. While the missionaries clearly functioned to facilitate the exploitation of Indian people, they themselves usually did not benefit from those acts of exploitation. . . . While the work of the missionaries helped to facilitate the political and economic exploitation of Indian people for the considerable benefit of the larger immigrant body politic, most had no interest in any significant personal profit. This might suggest naive innocence on their part. The direct support they provided to the white economic and political power structures would belie that assessment, however. At some level, they must have known what they were about.

Questions for Discussion

1. Who are the victims in these excerpts? Who are the villains? Are such judgments useful in interpreting the past?

2. Is genocide an appropriate word to apply to missionary efforts? To the settlers who came to the West in search of new opportunities? (See chapter ten for more information about genocide in the context of the Jewish Holocaust.)

3. Was the displacement and ultimate subjugation of the Indians inevitable? Was it necessary for the success of the American nation?

9

Dust, Depression, and the New Deal

Did the New Deal Provide Any Relief to Dust Bowl Farmers?

April 14, 1935, was Black Sunday on the southern Great Plains. The day had arrived with promise, clear and sunny, but in the afternoon the horizon filled suddenly with a massive dark cloud of blowing dust. Residents sought shelter as the dust storm surged across the region, blotting out the sun and enveloping towns as though they had been swallowed by the earth itself. The small farming communities that populated the region were by then accustomed to these dust storms, which had blown with increasing frequency since 1932, but the Black Sunday storm assailed them with theretofore unmatched ferocity. The following day Associated Press reporter Robert Geiger toured the area, and the dispatch he filed gave the windblown region its enduring name: "Three little words achingly familiar on a Western farmer's tongue, rule life in the dust bowl of the continent—if it rains." But it would not rain in any meaningful way until the end of the decade, and it was left to the farmers and the federal government to save the farms where nature, it seemed, would not.

Throughout the 1930s the farmers of the Dust Bowl region—a five-state area encompassing the Texas and Oklahoma panhandles, northeastern New Mexico, southeastern Colorado, and much of western Kansas—were buffeted by a combination of economic and natural hardships unparalleled in U.S. history. The misery of the

Great Depression was compounded by drought and the dust storms that literally blew away their livelihood, robbing the soil of its richness, clogging lungs, and silting into every crack and cranny. The federal government responded to their plight with a succession of New Deal programs designed to stabilize both the economy and the land.

Controversial in its own time, the successes and failures of the New Deal (and there is little consensus about which are which) continue to echo across the wheat fields, ranges, and grasslands of the southern Plains. Just how divisive the New Deal policies remain is illustrated by historians Donald Worster and Paul Bonnifield. Four decades after the dust settled, in books published in the same year with virtually identical titles, Worster and Bonnifield consider the role of the federal government in the Dust Bowl and come to vastly differing conclusions.

The Wheat Farmer and the Welfare State
Donald Worster

[The Dust Bowl community of Haskell County, Kansas] did accept other changes that made farming a very different enterprise from what it had been before the thirties. These other developments came from the federal government, and in their sum they amounted to a new welfare-state existence for the Haskell farmer, whether he was big or small, market-oriented or semisubsistent. The welfare state, created in the main by Roosevelt's New Deal, basically was a government that used its power and resources to protect people from getting trampled in the competitive jungle of free enterprise—the aged, the unemployed, the migrant workers. Farmers all over the country claimed, often justifiably, that they had much in common with those hapless victims and that Washington ought to be giving them a helping hand, too, so they themselves would not be ground under. So attentive were New Deal planners, as well as the President and Congress, to this plea that agriculture became one of the welfare state's most important concerns. In fact, saving the American farmer was, to many officials, the key to saving the entire society from Depression and injustice—"agricultural fundamentalism," the stance was termed, meaning help the farmers first and everyone would be better off. The people of Haskell

From Donald Worster, *Dust Bowl: The Southern Plains in the 1930s* (New York: Oxford University Press, 1979), 154-8, 161-3. Reprinted with permission.

County thoroughly agreed with that sense of priorities. Accepting the welfare state's support, however, involved a partial but significant substitution of the government office for the grain elevator and marketplace in the county's life.

It may seem ironic that wheat farmers in Kansas, who had become so fully a part of the economic system, would want protection from its penalties for failure. But the experiences of overproduction and dust storms were sufficiently traumatic to produce a revised maxim for business farming in the decade: do not interfere with us when we are making money, but rescue us when we are going bankrupt. To be sure, they were not alone in their fear of the root-hog-or-die ethic. As Undersecretary of Agriculture M. L. Wilson observed, "Underlying all the wants and needs of people today is an overwhelming desire for security"—which in translation read, put no ceiling over our heads, but build an income floor under our feet. Americans had tasted just enough affluence not to want to lose it, even where they were most devoted to a gambling way of life. The public cost of economic security, however, came high, in the case of agriculture amounting to about $1.4 billion a year by 1940. It was at that time the largest single item in the federal budget. That amount of various kinds of government assistance to the nation's farmers added, by A. Whitney Griswold's calculations, 10 per cent to the consumer's grocery bill. Clearly, farmers proved to be immensely successful in persuading the rest of the nation to pay for their protection, while, in the case of wheat entrepreneurs, preserving their self-aggrandizing ideology intact.

New Deal agriculture was the composite of too many individuals and programs to have a single end in view. For a large number of USDA bureaucrats the main goal was, as it had been since the 1920s, simply to enable the commercial farm sector to compete more successfully with manufacturing—to achieve the old parity level of rural purchasing power. To this circle, "agriculture" tended to become a monolithic abstraction; in their view all farmers, regardless of their size or assets, ought to be aided by subsidies, because all farmers labored at a disadvantage compared with their better organized industrial counterparts. In contrast, there were other officials who concentrated on the rural poor, of whom there were millions, and called for more directly targeted programs to help them survive. There was no end of conflict between the two groups. But running through much of the New Deal's agricultural thinking, as it did through Haskell County's, was a more unifying, if ambiguous, theme: the image and ideal of the family farm. An overwhelming majority of the country's 6 million farms were still family operations, although some of those families were considerably wealthier than others. A central ambition in the Roosevelt program was to keep as many families on the land as possible. The motives in that effort were, of course, not only undiscriminating, but parochial—to halt in this one area of the economy the movement toward concentration of power. Although the twentieth-century family farm was usually not the subsistence unit it had been in an earlier age, it still represented old hopes for preserving a virtuous, small-scale, decentralized society. New Dealers evoked a warm response from Americans whenever they talked of saving family-based agriculture, even if it meant, as M. L. Wilson admitted it might, the sacrifice of "maximum commercial productiveness." But that painful choice, he and others were confident, would not be required; the family farm could both operate as a modern, efficient business and also remain the country's chief defense against the corporate, industrial takeover. On the safeguarding of this traditional yet modernized agricultural institution, then, the welfare state expended much of its energy and imagination.

The defense was not limited to rhetorical flourishes; out in Haskell County many family farmers were indeed rescued from quicksand by government programs. The most important hands extended were those of the AAA and the rural rehabilitation campaign. In scale and community impact the Agricultural Adjustment Administration dwarfed everything else Washington did for the region. It was not designed specifically for the Dust Bowl; in fact, it aimed to do for the nation precisely what the southern plains through most of the thirties did not need to have done—cut back crop production instead of increasing it. Yet the AAA above all was a source of money, and plainsmen found that they could get it as readily as anyone.

After 1931, outside the drought states, American farmers continued to grow more wheat, corn, hogs, tobacco, and cotton than the markets could absorb, either at home or abroad; consequently, commodity prices sagged below operating expenses and stayed there. That ill-fed and ill-clothed people existed in the world, unable to enter the marketplace and bid on these products, was obvious. The AAA solution, however, was to concentrate on the producer's plight, not the would-be consumer's, by a plan of systematic, federally supervised decreases in leading commodities until supply matched "effective" (which is to say, backed up with cash) demand. "Planned scarcity," its critics called it—and they were absolutely right. But not being ready to restructure drastically the distribution of wealth in the United States, let alone in the world, Roosevelt's advisers decided that only a retrenchment policy could stave off a merciless economic war from which some Standard Oil of agriculture would emerge victorious, with power to control production and set prices wherever it chose. Established in the spring of 1933 to prevent that from happening, the AAA proved to be so immensely popular among farmers that something very like it had to be kept in action not only through the decade, but over the next forty years.

Although a cutback program was on the face of it absurd in a region where not much was growing, Haskell farmers did not waste time laughing. The government did not care whether your prospects for a crop were good or bad, so long as you agreed not to plant some of your fields. Haskell farmers therefore signed up *en masse*; 99 per cent of the county's operators—and in five townships it was 100 per cent—made contracts with the AAA by mid-September 1933. Under the terms of the contract they agreed to plant that fall, and for the next two years, only the acreage allowed them by Secretary of Agriculture Henry Wallace. . . . Only those who had seeded wheat in one or all of the preceding [three] years could qualify for the program. In exchange for leaving some of his ground idle, or putting it to some other use, the farmer earned a payment from Washington. But that was calculated according to the number of bushels of wheat he would probably harvest the next summer, a figure again derived from earlier yields. . . . Now came the higher mathematics: every wheat farmer was granted an allotment or share of the domestic market, which was 54 percent of the recent nationwide production. The AAA would pay only for these allotment bushels—that part of the harvest which would be consumed in the United States. Haskell's benefit payments were set in the 1933 contracts at 28 cents for each allotment bushel. In our hypothetical case, where the 54 percent allotment would equal 2066 bushels, the payment would come to $578. All of the farmer's wheat could be sold at the elevator, while at the same time he could draw this income supplement on the allotted bushels.

In a year like 1935, when 700 Haskell farmers harvested only 47,000 acres, or 67 acres apiece, there was a super-abundance of land on each farm that could be set aside, and little chance that anyone would try to work it surreptitiously. Nevertheless, committees that were appointed in each township traveled about to check on the accuracy of all allotments and acreages so that no one could defraud the government by reaping where, supposedly, he had not planted. The quantities of money involved made some kind of supervision necessary. During the first two years of AAA, Haskell collected just under $1 million in government wheat checks ("do not fold, perforate, or deface," they read), and in 1936 the average benefit received was $812 per operator. It was a tidy sum of cash for not doing a thing—more money, in fact, than millions of Americans could scrape together to live on each year, more money than a Haskell schoolteacher or minister might make. No wonder the county's farmers were outraged in January 1936, when the Supreme Court declared that the AAA's financing method—

a tax imposed on food processors—was unconstitutional. It was "the greatest economic disillusionment in the history of the county," complained the *Sublette Monitor.* Roosevelt immediately rushed through a replacement program, the Soil Conservation and Domestic Allotment Act, which paid farmers out of general revenues for following soil-building practices on surplus acreage instead of planting wheat or cotton. The AAA label, however, was too popular to abandon; in 1938 Congress passed a new Agricultural Adjustment Act with more complex acreage restrictions and benefit payments than ever, although the benefits were still paid directly by the federal treasury. Under the first of these two replacement programs Haskell County did not do as well as it had done, getting only $340,000 in 1937. But the sign-up rate was again 99 per cent in that year. Sensing that his constituents had abruptly opted for federal assistance, the Republican Congressman from the area, Clifford Hope, who had voted against the original AAA, leaped on the New Deal farm wagon with remarkable agility. With his help in redrawing the subsidies, the Haskell farmers took in $670,983 during 1939—compared with $641,064 they earned in the marketplace.

The subsidy-paying public assumed that for its money it was getting substantial crop reduction, but in fact the AAA and its successors—like the New Deal generally—did not go far enough to achieve its own goals. In 1933 Kansas cut its total wheat acreage not 15 per cent, but only 11.4. While almost all of the southwestern Kansas farmers signed contracts and followed them, those in the eastern part of the state saw that they would have a better chance if they stayed out of the federal programs. They had not been planting enough wheat in past years to qualify for high base acreages and allotments; now, with their competitors under restriction, they rushed in, hoping to grab the market. By 1936 Kansas had more wheat planted than it had had at any time in its history. Nationally, the wheat crop was temporarily reduced in the thirties, but that was due more to environmental distress than the government's measures. When those adverse conditions eased in 1938, wheat production soared to 962 million bushels, the second largest crop ever, and prices slid down again. Nor did all the New Deal subsidies really improve most farmers' position in the economy: in 1938 farm people constituted 25 per cent of the population, but they received, after several years of public assistance, only 8 percent of the national income, and as a whole they were slipping further behind each year. The AAA approach, whether right or wrong in what it attempted, fell far short of success. It did not improve the lot of the large number of poor, marginal farmers, nor did it control effectively the big, well-capitalized growers. . . .

The entry of these rural welfare programs into Haskell's life brought into being, in some ways, a new kind of agriculture. Every resident farmer became, under the pressure of circumstances, a unionist of sorts, working with those around him to keep afloat. . . . Many balked at all the advice and restrictions they suddenly had to submit to; it was often farm wives who proved most receptive to the changes and dragged their reluctant husbands to meetings. But community action and involvement among local farmers, although not an unfamiliar experience, took a big step forward during the 1930s, even if it largely amounted to pressure-group organizing.

As for saving the family farm, upon which Haskell rested so much of its hope, there was a mixed result. The names on the mailboxes, where there had been any, remained by and large the same through all the black blizzards and crop disasters. By decade's end the Snellbachers, Moores, Tatons, Preedys, and Blairs were still working the land as families, and they would go on doing so for some time to come. Haskell, therefore, had weathered, with outside support, its most trying years and had emerged with more continuity and stability than ever before. . . .

But there was a negative outcome too, which on balance was decisive. The threat to Haskell's social order came from something more than dust and drought: namely, all the disintegrative forces—attitudes as well as institutions—associated with commercial farming. In this frantic, hardscrabble period, when salvage, not expansion, was all that could be expected, the advance of large-scale business agriculture had come to a halt. But its underlying ethos—in particular, its devotion to extracting higher and higher profits out of the plains—merely lay dormant, ready to spring to life when the rains fell again. During this dormancy it was easier to talk about merging the business notion of success with the family farm ideal, but afterward such an amalgamation became far more problematic.

The Haskell farmer, observed Earl Bell in 1942, "believes himself to be as much a businessman as a manufacturer is." Yet somehow the farmer also expected to avoid the fate of family-owned and family-operated enterprises in the manufacturing world. Nothing in the AAA, which was government's major agricultural program, encouraged him to think differently. Nothing helped him to confront his basic dilemma: whether a business-run farm was truly compatible with traditional small-scale communal values. Nothing in any of the federal activities altered much the system of non-resident tenure, factory-like monoculture, and market speculation that had dominated the county. Not only did it fail to induce these changes, the emerging welfare state actually prevented their occurring. In the main it propped up an agricultural economy that had proved itself to be socially and ecologically erosive.

Men, Dirt, and Depression
Paul Bonnifield

In February 1934, the Agricultural Adjustment Administration instituted a submarginal land purchase program under authority provided in the National Industrial Recovery Act. The purchase of land continued under the Emergency Relief Appropriations Act of 1935 and other programs. . . .

Clearly the federal government was moving in the direction of comprehensive land-use planning, which would return vast acreages to grass, change the region's economy to stock raising, and reorganize the society of the dust bowl. These changes were viewed as necessary to correct serious national problems. What were the problems to be corrected? What caused the difficulty? Federal spokesmen for the National Resources Board and the Great Plains Committee believed that dramatic measures were necessary to rebalance agriculture, stop the loss of topsoil to wind erosion, and provide a marginal standard of living.

These spokesmen saw several causes for overproduction and soil waste. As a result of the Homestead Act and its later amendments, they said, farm size was too small. Interestingly, the impact of technology in shifting requirements in farm size received only casual consideration. The Homestead Act was also faulted for failing to restrict and rationalize land settlement along the lines of a preconceived plan. Since wheat was in great surplus, the planners saw wheat production as a primary cause of the disaster facing Great Plains farmers. They also argued that Great Plains farmers used methods of farming adapted to humid areas, that farming practices were deeply ingrained in the peoples' mind, and that they could not adjust to change without drastic measures being applied. The system of private land ownership was viewed as another cause of the disaster that stalked the Great Plains, as was unstable tenure on farms, especially with tenant farmers.

Having satisfied themselves as to the nature and the cause of the problems confronting the dust bowl farmers, spokesmen for comprehensive land-use planning put forward several proposals for solving the crisis. They believed that the federal government should purchase several million acres of land—from submarginal farms, tax delinquent lands, and sparsely settled areas. The acquired lands were to be added to federal and state public domain. Direct federal control over further acreages was to be expanded by lease, contract, formation of grazing

From Paul Bonnifield, *The Dust Bowl: Men, Dirt, and Depression* (Albuquerque: University of New Mexico Press, 1979), 114-6, 170-83. Reprinted with permission.

associations with private individuals, and expansion of grazing land under the Taylor Grazing Act [regulating livestock on the public domain].

Farm size was to be increased through "extension of credit under suitable restrictions." The minimum size for a family farm was to be determined and demonstration farms established to instruct the farmers in proper farming methods. Because of the "suitable restrictions" clause, and other aspects of the land-use plan, little credit was extended to farmers in the heartland of the dust bowl to expand their farm holdings.

To handle the excess farm population, and to prevent further settlement in sparsely settled areas, federal planners proposed several programs. The surplus population was to be resettled on subsistence farms. States were to restrict funds for roads and other governmental services in frontier regions. Private real estate dealers were to be licensed and regulated. Zoning laws, which would restrict settlement patterns and cropping practices, were to be passed. The zoning laws were seen as a primary means of controlling many aspects of agriculture and they revealed the desire to establish soil conservation districts, which would control the farming and grazing practices of the individual farmers. The regulatory capstone was the removal of English Common Law rights for private ownership. Land was to be owned by the public at large, with the federal government becoming the primary administrator and watchdog of the public interest. The entire program was to be directed through a closely coordinated series of local, state, and federal agencies, and the farmers were to be placed in a condition of pupilage. . . .

The new federal structure soon made itself felt by restricting farm loans, especially on wheat; however, loans were available for livestock raising. The new organization emphasized livestock raising by encouraging the construction of pit silos [underground storage for livestock feed] and range-improvement practices. To facilitate the exodus of people from certain areas, relief work was stopped. In Morton County, Kansas, a target area for land purchases, in a two-week period in August, after relief work was stopped, many people became refugees. Most of the families who moved hoped to return and reestablish their lives, but instead they became like characters in *The Grapes of Wrath*. . . .

The farmers in the five-state area were not ready to give up. They dealt a big blow to the scheme of reorganizing their society and drastically changing their land ownership by voting down the proposed Soil Conservation Districts. The shift in the decision-making power to an absentee landlord with extensive authority was more than the farmers would agree to. Many of the farmers had immigrated from nations where the land use was administered by the government, and they wanted no part of it in their new homeland. . . .

The advancement of soil conservation took a major step forward with the approval of state laws and county ordinances that required that idle land be properly protected from wind erosion. Most of the absentee landowners had simply left their land untouched, and these farms became severe menaces to neighboring fields and a primary source of wind erosion. With the passage of laws that required attention to the soil, and the subsequent attention given the abandoned fields, the erosive impact of the wind was significantly reduced.

The laws had an important side effect for the region. With the introduction of tractors, combines, one-way plows, and trucks, the most economical size of farm moved sharply upward. When the drought and depression struck the five-state area, the land ratio of farms was radically out of balance. A better balance in farm units occurred after the laws requiring soil maintenance were passed. Absentee landowners who were unable to care for their abandoned land, and still faced the cost of maintaining the soil, began leasing and selling their property to resident farmers. There was an infinite variety of land agreements, but overall, the land ratio to farm units and farmers was significantly improved. Land control adjustment of farm size was accomplished without major depopulation of the region. The adjustments necessary to meet the challenge of the changing technology occurred without extensively reorganizing the society and its culture. During the 1940s, "the boys that stuck it out did alright." The simple but practical solution of increasing the individual farmer's holdings and land control worked miracles in solving the vexing problem of farm size. While local farmers were making their adjustments for raising wheat, federal policy makers were plunging along a different line.

One of the primary reasons for turning the dust bowl back to grass was to find a permanent solution to the surplus production of wheat. By the government plan, eastern areas would raise wheat while western areas raised cattle. . . .

The Southwest Agricultural Association met in Guymon in July 1937 and approved a set of resolutions presented to Roy I. Kimmel [Resettlement Administrator and Federal Coordinator for the region]. The resolutions called for the implementation of several conservation practices and the creation of county committees with broad discretionary powers to assure that the conservation measures were practiced by individual farmers. The association agreed that wild lands should be returned to grass either through government purchase or private effort.

The primary difference between the position of the Southwest Agricultural Association resolutions and the position of the federal government was over what type of economy and society should exist in the dust bowl. The agricultural association wanted a community based on cultivation; the government wanted a pastoral system and government-planned agriculture. The two organizations also differed sharply over what constituted submarginal farms. The association based its definition on the soil while the government formed its definition from a host of conditions. . . .

The whole satiation of credit, farm programs, relief stoppages, government reports, and official statements caused the residents of the five-state region to look askance at the [federal] land purchase [program to return the dust bowl to grasslands]. To quiet the fears, government representatives began a series of local meetings. In Dalhart, Texas, J. C. Foster, Regional Director of the Land Utilization Division of the Bureau of Agricultural Economics explained that the "acreage sought is 'wild land,' not under lease or operation and which is or may be a wind erosion menace to adjacent land."

The request for the purchase of a tract of land for the Kiowa Grasslands in New Mexico by Felix E. Neff and others in 1938 was revealing when compared to Foster's statement. "It is considered to be very important," wrote Neff, "that such lands be purchased as soon as budgetary considerations will permit, in order that they may be brought under a system of management in conformity with the other lands within the project, and further, to forestall their future acquisition by small farmers." So they wanted to rush the purchase of land lest a private individual buy it first. A farmer who did not have a large enough unit to operate economically might decide to expand onto land desired by the government.

Foster stated that "the acreage sought was 'wild land' not under lease or operation . . ." Of the 91,173 acres sought in the Neff request, however, only 4,133 acres were abandoned. In fact, "emigration from this area is not as great as from other areas of this region." Thus Foster's statement and Neff's action are quite different. . . . The federal men wanted the land controlled under covenants to the landlord. Clearly, there was a vast difference between words and deeds. . . .

The tenor of the justifications for the eighteen parcels of land listed under the purchase request suggests that the government was busy establishing a big cow outfit. To gain control over water, the government was willing to pay the highest of prices. Not all the tracts of land suffered from wind erosion and only a few of the tracts could be described as wild. Of the eighteen tracts of land in the purchase, six were owned by the Federal Land Bank. And the federal purchasers were not above squeezing a farmer off his land. Part of the justification for the purchase of Tract No. 5115 from Claudia Martin was: "This tract should be purchased because it is a part of the operated unit which includes Tract 93. Tract 93 . . . should be taken out of crop production." The purchase request explained that an unidentified man owned Tract 93 and leased Tract 5115. It was strongly implied that by purchasing the farmer's leased land and breaking up the farming unit, the owner of Tract 93 would be forced to sell to the federal government.

The 110 acres of cultivated land on Tract No. 5115 in the Kiowa Grasslands was not seriously damaged by wind erosion. The purchase request claimed: "The soil is light loam and is *a potential menace* if crop cultivation is continued" (italics added). After eight years of continuous drought, with an average precipitation of 10.60 inches, and one year (1933) with only 4.88 inches of precipitation and strong winds, the cultivated lands in Union County that were inclined to blow had already blown. Apparently the term "potential danger" was a catchall phrase used to meet the soil conservation requirement for justifying land acquisitions. In the case of Tract No. 5115, potential danger was used to squeeze a man out of his home on Tract No. 93.

Land was purchased at the lowest dollar possible, regardless of poverty or needs of the seller. . . . When the farmer was the poorest and least capable of resisting pressure, the federal government paid the lowest price. These hardcore poor farmers were the submarginal farmers whom the government professed to help. . . .

The desires of the federal government to establish constructive conservation practices in the region was [*sic*] illuminated by the agencies responsible for establishing grasslands. In the spring of 1935 the Soil Conservation Service was established to promote conservation practices and to preserve our natural soil resources. Logically the Soil Conservation Service would have been held responsible for correcting the land misuse in the dust bowl and providing methods of controlling the erosion. Instead, the Resettlement Administration held primary responsibility for the soil conservation. The titles of the organizations and their position of responsibility suggest the government's goal. The Resettlement Administration was replaced by the Farm Security Administration followed by the Bureau of Agricultural Economics. Finally in November 1938, the grasslands came under the auspices of the Soil Conservation Service. The shift to the Soil Conservation Service marked a major shift in the federal government's experiment in land use and social reorganization along lines consistant [*sic*] with the general government leader's missionary spirit and desires to use the general public as specimens in a great laboratory for social experimentation. Yet, many of the folks who fell victim to the experiment carried its marks.

The national grasslands story of changing dustland to grassland was not a heroic effort by farsighted men who wished to undo the sins of the past and give the region the blessings of rebirth. It was a sad story of men inflicted with a missionary spirit and little understanding of the problems or their solutions.

Questions for Discussion

1. How did Franklin Roosevelt and the New Dealers respond to the Dust Bowl? What was their vision for agriculture on the southern Great Plains? Was the government solution effective?

2. How did people living in the stricken areas respond? What was their view of the New Deal programs? Was there anything they could have done to prevent the Dust Bowl?

3. Are farmers just businesspeople who substitute fields for factories? Should the federal government treat them as such? Or do farmers deserve a special measure of support and protection from the government? Why or why not?

4. Could anything (other than rain) have prevented or ameliorated the Dust Bowl? Does the environment impose limits on the development of society, or can these obstacles be overcome with the proper techniques and technologies?

5. How can two historians examining the same material at the same time come to such divergent conclusions? What does this suggest about the nature of historical research?

10

World War II

Why Didn't the United States Bomb Auschwitz?

More than six decades after the ovens of Auschwitz stopped burning, their smoke still hangs in the air. Over a million Jewish men, women, and children, and other "undesirables" were exterminated at the site, the largest and most efficient death camp in the Nazis' Final Solution. Today its ruins stand in the Polish countryside as a monument to the victims of the Holocaust and tangible reminders of the human capacity for hatred and cruelty magnified by the power of the modern state. To many, including Roger M. Williams, the remains of Auschwitz also symbolize a contemptible failure of compassion. Williams represents a group of scholars who ask why the United States and its allies did not do more to save Europe's Jews. From refusing to relax immigration quotas before the war to declining to use air power against Auschwitz, these historians indict the Allies for leaving innocent people to die at Hitler's hands. They highlight the anti-Semitism that was then widespread in the United States and suggest that in this shared prejudice Americans must confront a degree of complicity with the Nazis. Henry L. Feingold responds to these charges. He admits that, in retrospect, it is clear that rescue efforts might have saved lives, but he asks readers to consider the Allied decisions in the context of their times and in the context of a war that was, like every war, in many other ways also a war against the innocent.

By 1944 the Allies knew the truth about Auschwitz. In April 1944 two young Slovak men escaped from the camp and dictated a thirty-page report of what they knew about it, including its mass killing apparatus. A copy of their report reached the United States by June and began appearing in the press. Yet despite repeated requests from several officials within the Roosevelt administration and without, the military never bombed any of the rail lines leading to the camp, or otherwise used its air power to disrupt the killing. Military officials steadfastly maintained that such "rescue operations" would divert needed capacity away from the war effort, an effort that they contended would end the fighting faster and thus save more lives in the long run.

Although the Allies were aware of the killings at Auschwitz during the war, it wasn't until the German defeat in 1945 that the full scope of atrocities encompassed by the Nazi program of genocide (a word coined to denote the "destruction of a nation or of an ethnic group" attempted by the Nazis) came fully to light. After the war, the world recoiled with horror as Nazi officials on trial at Nuremberg detailed the workings of the Final Solution, and introspective observers asked not only how such brutality could come to pass but also why the world stood by while it did.

The unprecedented enormity of the evil at Auschwitz—the ferocious anti-Semitism of the Nazis and their partners, reducing mass murder to the banalities of modern mechanization—can overwhelm those who study it. A small group of pseudoscholars are so overpowered, or so unwilling to admit that Jews have been victims, that they simply deny that the Holocaust ever happened. But scholars more faithful to their historical profession probe the ruins at Auschwitz for insights that will equip us with the understanding and resolve to engage and prevent such atrocities in the future. These historians grapple with a range of emotions that include guilt, despair, and anger. Some invoke the moral authority of blame, while others seek to understand the actors of the past without passing judgment. The skeletal buildings at Auschwitz, still standing because the Allies refused to destroy them, also provoke deep and difficult questions about the nature and purpose of historical study. As you read the essays that follow, consider not only how Williams and Feingold approach the questions of Auschwitz, but what their answers suggest about the role of historians in our society.

Why Wasn t Auschwitz Bombed?
Roger M. Williams

In the spring and summer of 1944, the United States had its last major opportunity to act forcefully against Adolph Hitler's extermination of European Jews. Some five million Jews, as well as hundreds of thousands of other captives, had already been killed in pursuit of the Final Solution. At first disbelieving, then aghast but still largely indifferent, Americans and their government had watched the Final Solution unfold. Now, as Hitler moved in on Hungary, sending trainload after trainload of its Jews to their deaths in the gas chambers of Auschwitz, the United States again watched. By failing to intervene with bombs, rather than words, it sealed the fate of many thousands of innocent people. It also forfeited, yet again, this country's chance to stand as the conscience of the world in the face of unprecedented mass murder.

The issue aroused pitifully little interest at the time. Calling for bombing were a relatively small number of Jewish leaders, most of them rabbis, and a few civilian government officials who had no power to turn their views into policy and who were, in any event, not inclined to buck the dominant military apparatus. A sense of patriotism kept most questions of this kind from being asked, and the standard comeback "don't you know there's a war on?" was sure to stifle the rest. Bombing in behalf of Jews, the Department of War said curtly, would divert men and materiel needed to defeat the Axis; would needlessly risk American lives; and would, in any case, be "impracticable." So the proposals died quietly, along with the victims they were intended to save. . . .

The United States had the capability to put Auschwitz out of business, with miniscule damage to the war effort. What it lacked was the will—more basically, the concern. A strong case can be made for the feasibility and effectiveness of bombing several targets connected with the Hungarian episode of the Final Solution: Auschwitz, the most destructive of the death camps, and the rail lines leading to it; the Budapest railroad yards, where the victims were marshaled for the trip to the gas chambers; even Budapest itself, home of a frightened regime reluctantly doing the Nazis' bidding. Depending on how quickly the bombing was done, the lives of between 50,000 and 450,000 Jews might have been saved. . . .

In January 1944, however, Roosevelt did establish a War Refugee Board, an agency that would become, however tentatively, the only

From Roger Williams, "Why Wasn't Auschwitz Bombed?" *Commonweal* 105 (24 Nov. 1978): 746-51. Reprinted with permission.

administration advocate of bombing in behalf of the Jews. Formation of the WRB seemed to signal a major change in administration attitudes toward the Final Solution. In an executive order, the President announced the administration's intention "to take all measures within its power to rescue the victims of enemy oppression who are in imminent danger of death and otherwise afford such victims all possible relief and assistance consistent with successful prosecution of the war." Six days later, Secretary of the Treasury Henry Morgenthau, Jr., who had convinced Roosevelt to form the WRB, sought to underscore the new policy to one of the departments that could be expected to play a major role in implementing it. In a lengthy memo to the Assistant Secretary of War, John J. McCloy, Morgenthau declared, "The President stated . . . that the existing facilities of the State, Treasury and War Departments would be employed to furnish aid to Axis victims to the fullest extent possible." Morgenthau requested that the text of his memo be sent to appropriate theater commanders. That would seem to be a logical procedure, but it was never followed. Decisions on requests to bomb the death camps and their rail facilities were made wholly within the confines of the Pentagon. . . .

Less than two weeks after the Morgenthau memo, the War Department, ostensibly replying to a British government request for clarification, established the following policy: "It is not contemplated that units or individuals of the armed forces will be employed for the purpose of rescuing victims of enemy oppression unless such rescues are the direct result of military operations conducted with the objective of defeating the armed forces of the enemy.". . .

An unescorted 2,000-mile round trip over enemy territory [to Auschwitz and back to Allied bases in southern Europe] does indeed sound hazardous—except that American bombers already were making that very trip to attack oil refineries in southern Poland. During the last half of 1944, the bombers made a regular tour of targets in that area: Odertal, Blechammer North, Blechammer South, and Oswiecim . . . the Polish name for Auschwitz. At least four missions were flown against these targets, and two of them were in the late summer, when the Auschwitz crematoria were operating full blast in a final frenzy of extermination. Thus no appreciable "diversion" of military resources would have been needed to attack the Nazis' most destructive death camp. The American planes were virtually flying over it to bomb synthetic oil and rubber plants several miles from the camp. The first raid, on August 20, involved 127 Flying Fortresses (B-24's). (Stray bombs from the September raid actually struck the Auschwitz complex. According to a local newspaper, some 15 German soldiers and several dozen inmates and "civilian workers" were killed.) According to the official Army Air Force history, the raids together dropped 235 tons of bombs. Unloading several of those tons on the adjacent camp would have been, in the context of wartime expenditure, an undetectable loss. . . .

The War Department was never challenged on any of its assertions. Among the few people distressed by the anti-bombing decisions, none knew enough to challenge them. Public opinion remained somnolent throughout. Had Auschwitz's victims been predominantly Englishmen, and probably if they'd been gentiles of any nationality, powerful Americans would have urged bombing—and the government would have taken heed. Lucy Davidowicz, the historian, notes that the Allies also turned their backs on the Jews who revolted in the Warsaw ghetto, and she concludes soberly: "Helping Jews wasn't going to change anything with regard to the war. And nobody was willing to make it a 'Jewish war.' So they gave military excuses for what were really political reasons.". . .

One man, of course, could have singlehandedly brought bombs down on the death camps and their rail facilities. That was Franklin Roosevelt. It is, again, bitterly ironic that he, so castigated by his enemies as a friend of Jews, should have spurned the Jews in their time of greatest need. But Roosevelt bore the burden of the total war effort, and he lived in political fear [that his actions would be unpopular with the public and derided by opponents as] the 'Jew Deal.' In addition, he had the advice of his War Department that bombing in behalf of the Jews was "impracticable" and "of very doubtful feasibility." In John McCloy's recollection, Roosevelt had still another substantial question about the proposed action: "What would its psychological effect on the Germans be?"

McCloy explained recently: "A group of rabbis had been over to the White House, and the bombing issue came up. Harry Hopkins [Roosevelt's chief presidential assistant] came to me and said, 'What can you do about that? The rabbis think this will be spectacular, that it'll make front page headlines that will help the Jews, but we're not sure.' Hopkins and the President were worried about the reaction in Germany, whether bombing would stimulate even worse treatment of the Jews, with the Nazis simply murdering them out of hand."

In the end, Roosevelt did nothing, the War Department did nothing, and the Final Solution proceeded with no outside hindrances. At Auschwitz alone, almost half a million Jews died *after* the U.S. had acquired the ability to prevent their deaths there. Had Budapest's railroad marshaling yards been bombed in the spring, the mass deportations of Hungarian Jews might never have taken place. Had the city itself been severely bombed . . . the Hungarian puppet government might well have canceled the deportations long before it did; when [head of state] Admiral [Miklós] Horthy did cancel them, it was less than a week after the largest of the air raids on Budapest military targets. Had the rail lines leading to Auschwitz been bombed in late June, when that step was first proposed, roughly one-seventh of the Hungarian victims—more than 60,000 persons—could have been saved. And had Auschwitz been bombed in early October, when *that* was first proposed, somewhere around 50,000 could have been saved; according to sources in the European underground, that was the camp population at the time.

Just because Auschwitz and the rail facilities supporting it could easily have been bombed does not necessarily mean they should have been. Several other factors, some already mentioned and most involving the question of bombing accuracy, added complications. Considering them briefly, rail facilities first, then the camp:

Allied strategists in World War II argued long and hard about the efficacy of bombing rail targets. Some claimed that incessant attacks on rail centers would immobilize the German war machine; others, that broken track could be repaired, quickly and with relative ease and that such targets as oil refineries and armament factories therefore deserved priority. Germany's highly efficient railway system transported more than 2½ million people to their deaths between October 1941 and October 1944; "throughout that time," notes an authority on the German system, ". . . no Jew was left alive for lack of transport."

Yet it is far from certain, given his increasing difficulties in mid-1944, that Hitler would have committed the resources needed to keep in working order rail lines and marshaling yards far from either the Eastern or Western fronts. If the War Department thought railway bombing "of very doubtful efficacy," as McCloy wrote to [executive director of the War Refugee Board John W.] Pehle, its field operations did not reflect that judgment; despite uneven results, the Army Air Force continued bombing rail facilities right through the summer and fall of 1944. And since at least some of the lines leading northward to Auschwitz carried military personnel and supplies, it is difficult to understand why they weren't made targets on that basis alone. . . .

What about losses among the inmate population—killing the very people you were trying to save? Without question there would have been inmate deaths, perhaps dozens of them. Whether those deaths would have been justifiable in the process of rendering Auschwitz inoperable poses a difficult ethical question. Those who argued for bombing the camp obviously thought the answer to be yes, and I agree with them. Inmates of the Birkenau section, which would have been the prime target, were doomed in any event; I don't think it fanciful to suggest that their deaths would at least have had some purpose had they occurred as the mass extermination machinery was being destroyed. Besides, Allied air forces already were killing untold thousands of other innocents—slave laborers in German plants—without any apparent qualm.

It is often said that bombing would have been futile because the Nazis would have killed the captive Jews some other way. Indeed, Hitler's fanaticism in pursuit of the Final Solution can hardly be overestimated. But with Auschwitz inoperable and the war turning decidedly against him, the Führer might have neglected to take alternative steps needed to get the killing done. The Nazis had become impatient with their earlier forms of slaughter, like the forest massacre; that is why the gas chamber-crematoria combination so pleased Hitler and his deputy for death, [Adolph] Eichmann. It seems fair to assume that, if any of the suggested targets had been bombed, some and perhaps many lives would ultimately have been saved.

That point can be argued eternally. What appears beyond argument, a third of a century after those cataclysmic events, is that the bombing should have been done for larger symbolic reasons. Faced with the gigantic, systematic eradication of an entire people, the United States had a transcending moral obligation to act, and to act in a way that would be felt by the oppressor and honored by history. The worst sin was to do nothing but talk, because talk was powerless against the madness of the Final Solution.

Who Shall Bear Guilt for the Holocaust: The Human Dilemma
Henry L. Feingold

A simple searing truth emerges from the vast body of research and writing on the Holocaust. It is that European Jewry was ground to dust between the twin millstones of a murderous Nazi intent and a callous Allied indifference. It is a truth with which the living seem unable to come to terms. Historians expect that as time moves us away from a cataclysmic event our passions will subside and our historical judgment of it will mellow. But that tempered judgment is hardly in evidence in the historical examination of the Holocaust. Instead, time has merely produced a longer list of what might have been done and an indictment which grows more damning. There are after all six million pieces of evidence to demonstrate that the world did not do enough. Can anything more be said?

From Henry L. Feingold, *The Politics of Rescue: The Roosevelt Administration and the Holocaust, 1938-1945* (New York: Holocaust Library, 1980), 310-5, 318-21, 330. Reprinted with permission.

Yet there is some doubt whether characterizing the Holocaust witnesses as callously indifferent does full justice to historical reality. There is a growing disjuncture in the emerging history of the witness. We pile fact upon fact to demonstrate that almost nothing was done to save Jewish lives. Yet if the principal decision makers were alive today they would be puzzled by the indictment since they rarely thought about Jews at all. For them Auschwitz was merely a place name, for us it is a symbol of a civilization gone mad.

Historical research in the area of the Holocaust is beset with problems of no ordinary kind. It seems as if the memory of that man-made catastrophe is as deadly to the spirit of scholarship as was the actual experience to those who underwent its agony. The answers we are receiving are so muddled. The perpetrators have been found to be at once incredibly demonic but also banal. The suspicion that the victims were less than courageous, that they supposedly went "like sheep to the slaughter," has produced a minor myth about heroic resistance in the Warsaw ghetto and the forests of eastern Europe to prove that it wasn't so. Like the resistance apologetic, the indictment against the witnesses is as predictable as it is irresistible.

That is so because in theory at least witnessing nations and agencies had choices, and there is ample evidence that the choices made were not dictated by human concern as we think they should have been. . . .

The list of grievances is well known. The Roosevelt administration could have offered a haven between the years 1938 and 1941. Had that been done, had there been more largess, there is some reason to believe that the decision for systematic slaughter taken in Berlin might not have been made or at least might have been delayed. There could have been threats of retribution and other forms of psychological warfare which would have signaled to those in Berlin and in the Nazi satellites that the final solution entailed punishment. Recently the question of bombing the concentration camps and the rail lines leading to them has received special attention. The assumption is that physical intercession from the air might have slowed the killing process. American Jewry has been subject to particularly serious charges of not having done enough, of not using its considerable political leverage during the New Deal to help its brethren. Other witnesses also have been judged wanting. Britain imposed a White Paper limiting migration to Palestine in the worst of the refugee crisis, the Pope failed to use his great moral power against the Nazis, the International Red Cross showed little daring in interpreting its role vis-a-vis the persecution of the Jews. The list documenting the witnesses' failure of spirit and mind could be extended; but that would take us away from the core problem faced by the historian dealing with the subject. . . .

The question is, why did not the witnessing nations and agencies sense that the systematic killing in the death camps by means of production processes developed in the West was at the ideological heart of World War II, and therefore required a response? Why were they unable to fathom that Auschwitz meant more than the mass destruction of European Jewry? It perverted the values at the heart of their own civilization; if allowed to proceed unhampered, it meant that their world would never be the same again. Roosevelt, Churchill and Pius XII understood that they were locked in mortal combat with an incredibly demonic foe. But as the leaders of World War I sent millions to their death with little idea of the long-range consequences, these leaders never had the moral insight to understand that the destruction of the Jews would also destroy something central to their way of life. Even today few thinkers have made the link between the demoralization and loss of confidence in the West and the chimneys of the death camps. The Holocaust has a relatively low priority in the history texts used in our schools. It is merely another in a long litany of atrocities. Today as yesterday, few understand that a new order of events occurred in Auschwitz, and that our lives can never be the same again.

Yet how could it have been different? If the key decision makers at the time were told what Auschwitz really meant, would it have made a difference? They would have dismissed the notion that they could make decisions on the basis of abstract philosophy even if the long-range continuance of their own nations were at stake. They were concerned with concrete reality, with survival for another day. Until the early months of 1943 it looked to them as if their enterprise would surely fail. And if that happened, what matter abstract notions about the sanctity of life? The sense that *all* life, not merely Jewish life, was in jeopardy may have been less urgently felt in America, which even after Pearl Harbor was geographically removed from the physical destruction wrought by war. In America it was business as usual. What was being done to Jews was a European affair. Roosevelt viewed the admission of refugees in the domestic political context, the only one he really knew and could control to some extent. He understood that the American people would never understand the admission of thousands, perhaps millions, of refugees while "one third of the nation was ill housed, ill fed and ill clad." In case he dared forget, Senator Reynolds, a Democrat from North Carolina in the forefront of the struggle to keep refugees out, was there to remind him, and did so by using the President's own ringing phrases. . . .

A recent article in *Commentary* by Professor David Wyman and another by Roger M. Williams in *Commonweal* demonstrate beyond doubt that by the spring of 1944 the bombing of Auschwitz was feasible. Thousands of Hungarian and Slovakian Jews might have been saved had the American 15th Air Force, stationed in Italy and already bombing the synthetic oil and rubber works not five miles from the gas chambers, been allowed to do so. Moreover, by the fall of 1944 Auschwitz was well within the range of Russian dive bombers. Given that context, the note by Assistant Secretary of the Army John J. McCloy that bombing was of "doubtful efficacy" and the Soviet rejection of the idea are the most horrendously inhuman acts by witnesses during the years of the Holocaust. All that was required was a relatively minor change in the priority assigned to the rescue of Jews.

Yet a perceptive historian cannot long remain unaware of the seductive element in the bombing alternative. All one had to do, it seems, was to destroy the death chambers or the railroad lines leading to them, and the "production" of death would cease or at least be delayed. Things were not that simple. Jewish rescue advocates were late in picking up the signals emanating from Hungary for bombing, and even then there was little unanimity on its effectiveness. It was the World Jewish Congress which transmitted the request for bombing to the Roosevelt administration; but its own agent, A. Leon Kubowitzki, held strong reservations about bombing since he did not want the Jewish inmates of the camps to be the first victims of Allied intercession from the air. There was then and continues to be today genuine doubts that, given German fanaticism on the Jewish question and the technical difficulties involved in precision bombing, bombing the camps could have stopped the killing. The *Einsatzgruppen*, the special killing squads which followed behind German lines after the invasion of Russia, killed greater numbers in shorter order than the camps. The Germans were able to repair rail lines and bridges with remarkable speed. And, of course, Auschwitz was only one of the several camps where organized killing took place.

Most important, the bombing-of-Auschwitz alternative, so highly touted today, does not come to grips with the question of the fear that the Germans would escalate the terror and involve the Allies in a contest in which the Germans held all the cards. In a recent interview, McCloy cited this reason rather than the unwillinklgness to assign war resources to missions that were not directly involved in winning the war as the reason uppermost in Roosevelt's mind when the bombing alternative was rejected. An almost unnoticed sub-theme in McCloy's August 14th note spoke of the fear that bombing might "provoke even more vindictive action by the Germans." Survivors and rescue advocates might well wonder what "more vindictive action" than Auschwitz was possible. But that views the bombing alternative from the vantage of the Jewish victims—which, as we have seen, is precisely what non-Jewish decision makers could not do, given their different order of priorities and sense of what was possible. The people who conceived of the final solution could in fact have escalated terror. They could have staged mass executions of prisoners of war or of hostages in occupied countries or the summary execution of shot-down bomber crews for "war crimes." Their imagination rarely failed when it came to conceiving new forms of terror, nor did they seem to possess normal moral restraints as one might find in the Allied camp. That was one of the reasons why the final solution could be implemented by them. . . .

The behavioral cues of states came from within and were determined by the need of the organization to survive at all costs. With a few notable exceptions the rescue of Jews during the years of the Holocaust did not fit in with such objectives, and they were allowed to perish like so much excess human cargo on a lifeboat.

The indictment of the witnesses is based on the old assumption that there exists such a spirit of civilization, a sense of humanitarian concern in the world, which could have been mobilized to save Jewish lives during the Holocaust. It indicts the Roosevelt administration, the Vatican, the British government and all other witnessing nations and agencies for not acting, for not caring, and it reserves a special indignation for American Jewry's failure to mobilize a spirit which did not in fact exist.

Questions for Discussion

1. Why didn't the United States military bomb Auschwitz or the rail lines leading to the camp? Should it have? Did the U.S. fail the Jews of Europe? Does the refusal to divert air power for rescue operations implicate Roosevelt and other decision-makers in the tragedy?

2. Should historians make moral judgments about the people they study? Is this type of history—"why wasn't" and "what if"—helpful? Why or why not?

3. Do you think that the Jewish experience during the Holocaust was similar to the experience of American Indians during the eighteenth and nineteenth centuries? Were both instances of genocide, as George E. Tinker argues in chapter eight? Why or why not?

4. Compare Franklin Roosevelt's hesitation to focus on rescuing the Jews (as Commander-in-Chief of the military he could have ordered the bombing of Auschwitz, for instance) and Abraham Lincoln's hesitation to emancipate the slaves (see chapter six). How were their situations similar? Unique?

5. What similarities and differences do you see between the Holocaust and the more recent acts of genocide in Rwanda and Darfur, Sudan. Does the experience of World War II provide any useful lessons to apply in these cases, or does each stand alone as a unique situation?

11

The Civil Rights Movement

Free at Last?
Was Nonviolence the Best Strategy?

On December 1, 1955, in Montgomery, Alabama, a black woman named Rosa Parks refused to give up her seat on the bus to a white man, as Southern custom and Jim Crow segregation law dictated she should. Her small, unplanned act of defiance was the spark that ignited the Civil Rights Movement, a period that some historians have likened to a second Reconstruction in which black Americans asserted their claim to rights that had been promised but deferred since the Civil War. Yet over the next two decades the movement's leaders would divide over how best to assert that claim. Some followed Martin Luther King, Jr., in advocating a strategy of nonviolent protest. But as the movement made only limited progress, the more militant tactics promoted by Stokely Carmichael and the Black Panthers found an increasingly receptive audience.

The Reverend Martin Luther King, Jr., quickly emerged the most prominent figure in a boycott of the bus system in Montgomery, and as the movement expanded into a broad push for civil rights, he remained its most influential leader. King advocated a strategy of nonviolent protest influenced by Gandhi's example in India and rooted in his own Christian beliefs, organizing peaceful marches and demonstrations that were sometimes met with violence by the white authorities. King himself was arrested on several occasions, and it was during one of these imprisonments, in April 1963, that he wrote his "Letter From Birmingham Jail." The epistle is a response to criticisms from white clergy who supported King's cause but warned that the demonstrators were demanding change with undue haste, and it stands today as one of the most articulate expositions of the nonviolent protest ever set down on paper.

Under King's leadership the Civil Rights Movement became a major force in American culture and politics, but by the mid-1960s some black activists were dissatisfied with the slow pace of change and began advocating the more radical, potentially violent concept of Black Power as an antidote to white racism and cultural dominance. Stokely Carmichael, the recently elected and dynamic leader of the Student Nonviolent Coordinating Committee, was one of the most visible black leaders to reject nonviolent principles and the goal of integration. Carmichael popularized the concept of Black Power, calling for an all-black movement aimed at creating a separate place in American society. His "Free Huey" speech of 1968 came in the midst of a campaign to release the Black Panther leader Huey Newton from prison in California, where Newton was being held on charges of killing an Oakland police officer.

These two leaders represent the divergent ideologies of the Civil Rights Movement. Each is also more broadly connected to distinct philosophies of social change with deep roots in the American experience. King stood for civil disobedience, a form of protest with a long tradition in the nation's history, from Thoreau's protest of the war with Mexico to the antiwar activism of the times. Carmichael's belief in Black Power reflects a different tradition: oppressed people seeking to secure "by any means necessary"—including violence—the "unalienable" rights promised to all Americans.

Letter From Birmingham Jail
Martin Luther King, Jr.

April 16, 1963

In any nonviolent campaign there are four basic steps: collection of the facts to determine whether injustices exist; negotiation; self purification; and direct action. We have gone through all these steps in Birmingham. There can be no gainsaying the fact that racial injustice engulfs this community. Birmingham is probably the most thoroughly

From Martin Luther King, Jr., "Letter From Birmingham Jail" (April 16, 1963), available at http://www.stanford.edu/group/King/popular_requests/frequentdocs/birmingham.pdf. Reprinted with permission of Coretta Scott King.

segregated city in the United States. Its ugly record of brutality is widely known. Negroes have experienced grossly unjust treatment in the courts. There have been more unsolved bombings of Negro homes and churches in Birmingham than in any other city in the nation. These are the hard, brutal facts of the case. On the basis of these conditions, Negro leaders sought to negotiate with the city fathers. But the latter consistently refused to engage in good faith negotiation.

Then, last September, came the opportunity to talk with leaders of Birmingham's economic community. In the course of the negotiations, certain promises were made by the merchants—for example, to remove the stores' humiliating racial signs. On the basis of these promises, the Reverend Fred Shuttlesworth and the leaders of the Alabama Christian Movement for Human Rights agreed to a moratorium on all demonstrations. As the weeks and months went by, we realized that we were the victims of a broken promise. A few signs, briefly removed, returned; the others remained.

As in so many past experiences, our hopes had been blasted, and the shadow of deep disappointment settled upon us. We had no alternative except to prepare for direct action, whereby we would present our very bodies as a means of laying our case before the conscience of the local and the national community. Mindful of the difficulties involved, we decided to undertake a process of self-purification. We began a series of workshops on nonviolence, and we repeatedly asked ourselves: "Are you able to accept blows without retaliating?" "Are you able to endure the ordeal of jail?". . .

You may well ask: "Why direct action? Why sit-ins, marches and so forth? Isn't negotiation a better path?" You are quite right in calling for negotiation. Indeed, this is the very purpose of direct action. Nonviolent direct action seeks to create such a crisis and foster such a tension that a community which has constantly refused to negotiate is forced to confront the issue. It seeks so to dramatize the issue that it can no longer be ignored. My citing the creation of tension as part of the work of the nonviolent resister may sound rather shocking. But I must confess that I am not afraid of the word "tension." I have earnestly opposed violent tension, but there is a type of constructive, nonviolent tension which is necessary for growth. Just as Socrates felt that it was necessary to create a tension in the mind so that individuals could rise from the bondage of myths and half-truths to the unfettered realm of creative analysis and objective appraisal, so must we see the need for nonviolent gadflies to create the kind of tension in society that will help men rise from the dark depths of prejudice and racism to the majestic heights of understanding and brotherhood.

The purpose of our direct action program is to create a situation so crisis packed that it will inevitably open the door to negotiation. I therefore concur with you in your call for negotiation. Too long has our beloved Southland been bogged down in a tragic effort to live in monologue rather than dialogue. . . .

We know through painful experience that freedom is never voluntarily given by the oppressor; it must be demanded by the oppressed. Frankly, I have yet to engage in a direct action campaign that was "well timed" in the view of those who have not suffered unduly from the disease of segregation. For years now I have heard the word "Wait!" It rings in the ear of every Negro with piercing familiarity. This "Wait" has almost always meant "Never." We must come to see, with one of our distinguished jurists, that "justice too long delayed is justice denied."

We have waited for more than 340 years for our constitutional and God given rights. The nations of Asia and Africa are moving with jet-like speed toward gaining political independence, but we still creep at horse and buggy pace toward gaining a cup of coffee at a lunch counter. Perhaps it is easy for those who have never felt the stinging darts of segregation to say, "Wait." But when you have seen vicious mobs lynch your mothers and fathers at will and drown your sisters and brothers at whim; when you have seen hate filled policemen curse, kick and even kill your black brothers and sisters; when you see the vast majority of your twenty million Negro brothers smothering in an airtight cage of poverty in the midst of an affluent society; when you suddenly find your tongue twisted and your speech stammering as you seek to explain to your six-year-old daughter why she can't go to the public amusement park that has just been advertised on television, and see tears welling up in her eyes when she is told that Funtown is closed to colored children, and see ominous clouds of inferiority beginning to form in her little mental sky, and see her beginning to distort her personality by developing an unconscious bitterness toward white people; when you have to concoct an answer for a five-year-old son who is asking: "Daddy, why do white people treat colored people so mean?"; when you take a cross-county drive and find it necessary to sleep night after night in the uncomfortable corners of your automobile because no motel will accept you; when you are humiliated day in and day out by nagging signs reading "white" and "colored"; when your first name becomes "nigger," your middle name becomes "boy" (however old you are) and your last name becomes "John," and your wife and mother are never given the respected title "Mrs."; when you are harried by day and haunted by night by the fact that you are a Negro, living constantly at tiptoe stance, never quite knowing what to expect next, and are plagued with inner fears and outer resentments; when you are forever fighting a degenerating sense of "nobodiness"—then you will understand why we find it difficult to wait. There comes a time when the cup of endurance runs over, and men are no longer willing to be plunged into the abyss of despair. I hope, sirs, you can understand our legitimate and unavoidable impatience.

You express a great deal of anxiety over our willingness to break laws. This is certainly a legitimate concern. Since we so diligently urge people to obey the Supreme Court's decision of 1954 [*Brown v. Board of Education of Topeka*] outlawing segregation in the public schools, at first glance it may seem rather paradoxical for us consciously to break laws. One may well ask: "How can you advocate breaking some laws and obeying others?" The answer lies in the fact that there are two types of laws: just and unjust. I would be the first to advocate obeying just laws. One has not only a legal but a moral responsibility to obey just laws. Conversely, one has a moral responsibility to disobey unjust laws. I would agree with St. Augustine that "an unjust law is no law at all." Now, what is the difference between the two? How does one determine whether a law is just or unjust? A just law is a man made code that squares with the moral law or the law of God. An unjust law is a code that is out of harmony with the moral law. To put it in the terms of St. Thomas Aquinas: An unjust law is a human law that is not rooted in eternal law and natural law. Any law that uplifts human personality is just. Any law that degrades human personality is unjust. All segregation statutes are unjust because segregation distorts the soul and damages the personality. . . .

I hope you are able to see the distinction I am trying to point out. In no sense do I advocate evading or defying the law, as would the rabid segregationist. That would lead to anarchy. One who breaks an unjust law must do so openly, lovingly, and with a willingness to accept the penalty. I submit that an individual who breaks a law that conscience tells him is unjust, and who willingly accepts the penalty of imprisonment in order to arouse the conscience of the community over its injustice, is in reality expressing the highest respect for law.

Of course, there is nothing new about this kind of civil disobedience. It was evidenced sublimely in the refusal of Shadrach, Meshach and Abednego to obey the laws of Nebuchadnezzar [and were thus sentenced to be burned to death but were spared through divine protection, according to the Biblical story in Daniel chapter 3], on the ground that a higher moral law was at stake. It was practiced superbly by the early Christians, who were willing to face hungry lions and the excruciating pain of chopping blocks rather than submit to certain unjust laws of the Roman Empire. To a degree, academic freedom is a reality today because Socrates practiced civil disobedience. In our own nation, the Boston Tea Party represented a massive act of civil disobedience.

We should never forget that everything Adolf Hitler did in Germany was "legal" and everything the Hungarian freedom fighters did in Hungary was "illegal." It was "illegal" to aid and comfort a Jew in Hitler's Germany. Even so, I am sure that, had I lived in Germany at the time, I would have aided and comforted my Jewish brothers. If today I lived in a Communist country where certain principles dear to the Christian faith are suppressed, I would openly advocate disobeying that country's antireligious laws. . . .

I stand in the middle of two opposing forces in the Negro community. One is a force of complacency, made up in part of Negroes who, as a result of long years of oppression, are so drained of self respect and a sense of "somebodiness" that they have adjusted to segregation; and in part of a few middle-class Negroes who, because of a degree of academic and economic security and because in some ways they profit by segregation, have become insensitive to the problems of the masses. The other force is one of bitterness and hatred, and it comes perilously close to advocating violence. It is expressed in the various black nationalist groups that are springing up across the nation, the largest and best known being Elijah Muhammad's Muslim movement. Nourished by the Negro's frustration over the continued existence of racial discrimination, this movement is made up of people who have lost faith in America, who have absolutely repudiated Christianity, and who have concluded that the white man is an incorrigible "devil."

I have tried to stand between these two forces, saying that we need emulate neither the "do nothingism" of the complacent nor the hatred and despair of the black nationalist. For there is the more excellent way of love and nonviolent protest. I am grateful to God that, through the influence of the Negro church, the way of nonviolence became an integral part of our struggle.

If this philosophy had not emerged, by now many streets of the South would, I am convinced, be flowing with blood. And I am further convinced that if our white brothers dismiss as "rabble rousers" and "outside agitators" those of us who employ nonviolent direct action, and if they refuse to support our nonviolent efforts, millions of Negroes will, out of frustration and despair, seek solace and security in black nationalist ideologies—a development that would inevitably lead to a frightening racial nightmare.

Oppressed people cannot remain oppressed forever. The yearning for freedom eventually manifests itself, and that is what has happened to the American Negro. Something within has reminded him of his birthright of freedom, and something without has reminded him that it can be gained. Consciously or unconsciously, he has been caught up by the Zeitgeist, and with his black brothers of Africa and his brown and yellow brothers of Asia, South America and the Caribbean, the United States Negro is moving with a sense of great urgency toward the promised land of racial justice. If one recognizes this vital urge that has engulfed the Negro community, one should readily understand why public demonstrations are taking place. The Negro has many pent up resentments and latent frustrations, and he must release them. So let him march; let him make prayer pilgrimages to the city hall; let him go on freedom rides—and try to understand why he must do so. If his repressed emotions are not released in nonviolent ways, they will seek expression through violence; this is not a threat but a fact of history. So I have not said to my people: "Get rid of your discontent." Rather, I have tried to say that this normal and healthy discontent can be channeled into the creative outlet of nonviolent direct action.

Free Huey
Stokely Carmichael

Oakland, California
February 17, 1968

Survival means that we organize politically, we organize consciously (that's what [white people] call education; we call it black consciousness, because that speaks to us, education speaks to them), we organize economically, and we organize militarily. If we don't do that, if you don't have a gun in your hand, they can snatch the ballot from you. But if you have a gun, it's either them or us. The preparation of that fight on all levels must become conscious among our people. We are ahead of the Jews in Germany because we know what they're getting ready to do. They tell us every day in the *Esquire* magazines, they tell us on their televisions, they tell us with the 15,000 soldiers they're putting in the cities, they tell us with their tanks, they tell us with their Stoner guns,* they tell us! We must wake up and tell them *we* are going to get them.

Wipe the questions of minority and technology out of your mind. Technology never decides a war, it is the will of a people that decides a war. Wipe out of your mind the fact that we do not have guns. The Vietnamese didn't have guns when they started, now they have American guns, American tanks, American everything. If they come to get

---

*Special high-powered guns that can send bullets through brick walls ten feet thick; used as heavy duty police weapons.

From Stokely Carmichael, "Free Huey," in Ethel N. Minor, ed., *Stokely Speaks: Black Power to Pan-Africanism* (New York: Random House, 1971), 123-8. Reprinted with permission.

us they will have to bring some. We are going to take the gun, and
the tank, and the grenade! Unless we raise our minds to the level of
consciousness where we have an undying love for our people, where
we're willing to shed our blood like Huey Newton did for our people,
we will not survive. There are many people who know that. All of the
brothers sitting on the stage, all of the brothers around here [Black
Panthers] know that when something goes down, we are the first one
offed. There's no question in any of our minds. Only thing going to
stop us today is a bullet, and we are spittin' them back! The question
is not whether or not we can move, but how this entire black community moves for survival in a world that's clearly heading for a color
clash. That is what we must ask ourselves, the only question. We can
do that only by organizing our people and orienting them toward an
African ideology that speaks to our blackness—nothing else.

It's not a question of right or left, it's a question of black. You dig
where we are coming from? We are coming from a black thing, from
a *black* thing, that's where we are coming from. We can begin to pick
up the threads of resistance that our ancestors laid down for us. And
unless we begin to understand our people as a people, we will not do
that, because they *will* split us and divide us. That means consciously
we have to begin to *organize our people!* Nothing else! We have no
time for them; all our sweat, all our blood, even our life must go to
our people, nothing else. We have to understand this consciously. Our
youth must be organized with a revolutionary prospectus. A revolutionary prospectus says that we're fighting a war of liberation. In order
to fight a war of liberation, you need an ideology of nationalism. We
do not have this country. The nationalism can be nothing but black
nationalism. It is insane to think of anything else. Black nationalism
must be our ideology. While blackness is necessary, it is not sufficient,
so we must move on to consciously organize our communities. And
we recognize today while we're organizing that we do not have the
money to feed our people, so there's no use saying, "Organize, we can
get you a job." We can't get them, they control them, that is a fact.
That isn't a reason for you to sit down, it is only more reason for you
to fight. That's more of an inspiration to fight so you *can* give them
a job rather than to sit down and say the honkies have us on every
end. They are not God. We are a beautiful race of people, we can do
anything we want to do; all we have to do is get up, get up, get up
and do it!

We have to discuss very coldly the question of rebellions. It is a fact
that they're prepared to meet rebellions anywhere in the cities. Now,
what's going to happen if one of our brothers gets offed? What hap-
pens if they go ahead and off Huey Newton? We must develop tactics
where we do the maximum damage to them with minor damage to

us. When we move into the arena, that means that this black community must be organized [so] if Brother Huey Newton goes, and ten honky cops go, won't a black man in this community get up and open his mouth, because if he does, *he* goes too. That means that in organizing for the maximum damage against them and minor damage to us, we must be consciously aware of the fact that there will be people in our community who are going around doing just that. In our community, we see nothing, we hear nothing, we know nothing. . . .

Our people have demonstrated a willingness to fight. Our people have demonstrated the courage of our ancestors—to face tanks, guns, and police dogs with bricks and bottles. That is a courageous act! Since our people have demonstrated a willingness to fight, the question is how we can organize that fight so we win. If a major rebellion breaks out, our people may or may not become the losers, but if a small group was doing maximum damage, we remain on top. We remain on top. It is not a matter of *what* they might do, but only one of *how* and *when* they're going to do it. That is all. For us the question is not going to Vietnam any more, the question is how we can protect our brothers who do not go to Vietnam from going to jail so that when one brother says "Hell, no," there're enough people in that community around him, so that if they dare come in, they are going to face maximum damage in their community.

We are talking about survival. We are talking about a people whose entire culture, whose entire history, whose entire way of life have been destroyed. We're talking about a people who have produced in *this* year a generation of warriors who are going to restore to our people the humanity and the love that we have for each other. That's what we're talking about *today*, we are talking about becoming the executioners of our executioners. For example, you should give a lot of money to the Huey defense fund, because while some of that money will go for that court thing, the rest of the money's going for the executioners. If they execute Huey, the final execution rests in our hands.

It is simply a question of a people. They control everything. They make us fight, they make us steal, they judge us, they put us in prison, they parole us, they send us out, they pick us up again—where in God's name do we exercise any sense of dignity in this country? What in God's name do we control, except the church, whose ideology is set up to be compatible with the system that's against us? Where in God's name do we exercise any control as a people whose ancestors were the proudest people that walked the face of this earth? Everywhere the white man has gone he controls our people; in South Africa he steals the gold from our people, in the West Indies he steals the materials from our people, in South America, where he's scattered our people, he's raping us blind. He rapes us in America and in Nova Scotia. Where in God's name will we find a piece of earth that belongs to us so we can restore our humanity? Where will we find it unless this generation begins to organize to fight for it?

When this generation begins to fight, there can be no disruptive elements in our community. We will tolerate none. We put our lives on the line for anyone who fights for our people. Huey Newton fought for our people. Whether or not Huey Newton becomes free depends upon black people, nobody else. Other people may help, but the final decision on Brother Huey depends on *us*. He didn't lay down his life for other people, he laid it down for *us*. And if he did that, we must be willing to do the same, not only for him but for the generation that's going to follow us. . . .

We have to understand the politics of those honkies in our community. They are there to patrol and to control. Well, we are going to do the patrolling and controlling. We are building a concept of peoplehood. If the honkies get in our way, they will have to go. We are not concerned about their way of life, we are concerned about our *people*. We want to give our people the dignity and humanity that we once knew as a people, and if they get in our way, they're going to be offed. We're not concerned with their system. Let them have it. We want our way of life, and we're going to get it. We're going to get it or nobody's going to have any peace on this earth.

Questions for Discussion

1. What are the best ways to effect social change in the United States? Did nonviolence work during the Civil Rights Movement? If not, could it have worked over the course of time? Was militancy a legitimate solution, or did it intensify the problem?

2. Overall, what did the Civil Rights Movement achieve? Have black Americans finally realized the promises of liberty and equality, or is the racial reconstruction of the nation an ongoing process?

3. In what ways is identity tied to race or ancestral origins? In what ways is it an achievement that individuals must work out for themselves? Do you see any similarities between the issues of racial identity raised by black Americans during the Civil Rights Movement and other groups in other periods from American history?

12

The Vietnam War

Did the Press Undermine the United States Military in Vietnam?

Before World War II was over, keen observers noticed a new conflict emerging. As victory drew near, the United States and its wartime ally, the USSR, began to jockey for position and influence on the postwar landscape. In the decades to come, the Soviets looked to export their brand of communism to other countries while the U.S. pursued a policy of containment (which itself involved some exportation of the American system). Although the two superpowers generally avoided direct confrontation (with the notable exception of the Cuban Missile Crisis in 1962), in several places they fought through surrogates. Every time these Cold War battlegrounds flashed hot, the American media brought the conflict home to a news-hungry public.

From the U.S. perspective, the most notable of these engagements was Vietnam (or Viet Nam, as it is sometimes spelled in English). Americans at home followed the war through an unprecedented variety of media outlets—they could read about the latest events in the morning newspapers, get more comprehensive analysis of the war effort from newsmagazines like *Time* and *Newsweek*, and (most novel of all) watch footage from the war zone on the television evening news. So central was the media to the public's perception of the war that when it became controversial at home, the Vietnam press corps also drew criticism. A few observers, such as veteran Vietnam correspondent Robert Elegant, felt that the media presented the war with an undue negative bias that turned public opinion against U.S. military involvement. A number of others, like *New York Times* correspondent Charles Mohr, have defended the press corps's performance in Vietnam. Mohr points to the reporting on complicated events like North Vietnam's Tet offensive to show that, while mistakes were inevitably made, on the whole the media maintained an admirable standard of objectivity.

While the role of the media as an intentional antagonist is open to debate, it is clear that after Tet the war increasingly divided American society. Massive protests and counterprotests rocked campuses and cities throughout the nation as the press kept up a drumbeat of increasingly negative news out of Vietnam. As the war effort seemed to turn against the U.S. and opposition mounted at home, many people, including General William Westmoreland, commander of American military operation in Vietnam, complained that the "hostile" media was undercutting the war effort and snatching defeat from the jaws of victory. Even today the war remains a raw point of contention in the public discourse, as journalists, historians, generals, presidents, and others continue to debate not only the press's impact on the Vietnam War effort but also its role in the nation's more recent wars.

How to Lose a War
Robert Elegant

In the early 1960's, when the Viet Nam War became a big story, most foreign correspondents assigned to cover the story wrote primarily to win the approbation of the crowd, above all their own crowd. As a result, in my view, the self-proving system of reporting they created became ever further detached from political and military realities because it instinctively concentrated on its own self-justification. The American press, naturally dominant in an "American war", somehow felt obliged to be less inspired by the *engagé* "investigative" reporting that burgeoned in the US in these impassioned years. The press was instinctively "agin the Government"—and, at least reflexively, for Saigon's enemies.

During the later half of the 15-year American involvement in Viet Nam the media became the primary battlefield. Illusory events reported *by* the press as well as real events *within* the press corps were

From Robert Elegant, "How to Lose a War: Reflections of a Foreign Correspondent," *Encounter* (United Kingdom) 57, no 2 (August 1981): 73-91. Reprinted with permission.

more decisive than the clash of arms or the contention of ideologies. For the first time in modern history, the outcome of a war was determined not on the battlefield, but on the printed page and, above all, on the television screen. Looking back coolly, I believe it can be said (surprising as it may still sound) that South Vietnamese and American forces actually won that limited military struggle. They virtually crushed the Viet Cong in the South, the "native" guerrillas who were directed, reinforced, and equipped from Hanoi; and thereafter they threw back the invasion by regular North Vietnamese divisions. None the less, the War was finally lost to the invaders *after* the US disengagement because the political pressures built up by the media had made it quite impossible for Washington to maintain even the minimal material and moral support that would have enabled the Saigon regime to continue effective resistance. . . .

Television, its thrusting and simplistic character shaping its message, was most shocking because it was most immediate. The Viet Nam War was a presence in homes throughout the world. Who could seriously doubt the veracity of so plausible and so moving witness in one's own livingroom?

At any given moment, a million images were available to the camera's lens in Saigon alone—and hundred of millions throughout Indo-China. But TV crews naturally preferred the most dramatic. That, after all, was their business—show business. It was not news to film farmers peacefully tilling their rice-fields, though it might have been argued that nothing happening *was* news when the American public had been led to believe that almost every Vietnamese farmers was regularly threatened by the Viet Cong, constantly imperilled [*sic*] by battle, and rarely safe from indiscriminate US bombing.

A few hard, documented instances. A burning village was news, even though it was a deserted village used in a Marine training exercise—even though the television correspondent had handed his Zippo lighter to a non-commissioned officer with the suggestion that he set fire to an abandoned house. American soldiers cutting ears off a Viet Cong corpse was news—even if the cameraman had offered the soldiers his knife and "dared" them to take those grisly souvenirs. (Since the antics of the media were definitely *not* news, the network refrained from apologising for the contrived "event" when a special investigation called the facts to its attention.) Cargo-nets full of dead South Vietnamese soldiers being lowered by helicopters were news—even if that image implicitly contradicted the prevailing conviction that the South Vietnamese never fought, but invariably threw away their weapons and ran.

The competition in beastliness among the networks was even more intense than the similar competition among the representatives of the print media. Only rarely did television depict peaceful fields in which water buffaloes pulled ploughs for diligent farmers—undisturbed by air-bursts, rockets, infantrymen, or guerrillas. One special report *was*, however, devoted largely to depicting bucolic scenes and untravelled roads when Prince Norodom Sihanouk invited a television correspondent to tour the border areas of Cambodia to prove that his country was *not* being used by the North Vietnamese as a base for operations against South Viet Nam. A few years later, Sihanouk of course acknowledged that the North Vietnamese *had* at the time been—and had remained—intensely active in precisely those areas. But television could "prove" either a negative or a positive proposition—depending on where the camera pointed and upon the correspondent's inclination. . . .

In fairness, a number of newspaper correspondents also endorsed Sihanouk's contention that there were no North Vietnamese soldiers in Cambodia. Since the correspondents had seen no invaders, there were, patently, no invaders to be seen. The assumption of omniscience that lay behind so much of the coverage of Indo-China remains awe-inspiring. . . .

Nowadays, [reporters] Jen Lacouture, Anthony Lewis, and William Shawcross (among some other "Viet Nam veterans") clearly feel deceived or even betrayed by the Communists of Indo-China; yet surely, they voluntarily adopted the ideological bias that allowed Hanoi to deceive them. The Vietnamese Communists—unlike their Cambodian confrères—had, after all, openly *declared* their intention of imposing totalitarian rule upon the South. Why, then, were the "critics of the American war" so genuinely surprised by the consequences? More crucially, why did a virtual generation of Western journalists deceive itself so consistently as to the nature of the "liberation" in Indo-China? Why did the correspondents *want* to believe in the good faith of the Communists? Why did they so *want* to disbelieve the avowed motives of the United States? Why did so much of their presumably factual reporting regularly reflect their ideological bias?

The obvious explanation is not as ingenuous as it may appear: the majority of Western correspondents and commentators adopted their idiosyncratic approach to the Indo-China War precisely because other journalists had already adopted that approach. To put it more directly, it was fashionable (this was, after all, the age of Radical Chic) to be "a critic of the American war."

Decisive in the case of the Americans, who set the tone, was the normally healthy adversary relationship between the US press and the US government. American newspapermen have often felt, with some justification, that if an Administration affirmed a controversial fact, that fact—if not *prima facie* false—was at the least suspect. As the lies of successive Administrations regarding Indo-China escalated, that conviction became the credo of the press. The psychological process that began with the unfounded optimism of President John F. Kennedy's ebullient New Frontiersmen, who were by and large believed, ended with the disastrous last stand of Richard Nixon's dour palace guard, who were believed by no one.

The reaction against official mendacity was initially healthy, but later became distorted, self-serving, and self-perpetuating. A faulty syllogism was unconsciously accepted: Washington was lying consistently; Hanoi contradicted Washington; therefore Hanoi was telling the truth.

The initial inclination to look upon Hanoi as a fount of pure truth was intelligently fostered by the Communists, who selectively rewarded "critics of the American war" with visas to North Viet Nam. A number of influential journalists and public figures (ranging from former cabinet officers to film actresses) were fêted in North Viet Nam. They were flattered not only by the attention and the presumed inside information proffered by the North Vietnamese, but by their access to a land closed to most Americans. The favoured few—and the aspiring many—helped establish a climate in which it was not only fashionable but, somehow, an act of courage to follow the critical crowd in Saigon and Washington while praising Hanoi. The sceptical [*sic*] correspondent risked ostracism by his peers and conflicts with his editors if he did not run with "the herd of independent minds," if he did not support the consensus. . . .

The main question persists. Why was the press—whether in favour of official policy at the beginning or vehemently against the War at the end—so superficial and so biased?

Chief among many reasons was, I believe, the politicisation of correspondents by the constantly intensifying clamour over Viet Nam in Europe and America. Amateur (and professional) propagandists served both sides of the question, but the champions of Hanoi were spectacularly more effective. They created an atmosphere of high pressure that made it exceedingly difficult to be objective. . . .

Many newcomers were shocked to find that American and Vietnamese briefing officers did not always tell them the truth even about a minor tactical situation. Despite their pose of professional skepticism, in their naivety they expected those officers to tell not merely the truth, but the *whole* truth. Far from feeling the deep mistrust of officialdom they affected, the newcomers were dismayed by the briefing officers' inability (or unwillingness) to confide in them unreservedly. Older correspondents did not expect candour from briefing officers. They had learned several wars earlier that the interests of the Press and the interests of the Military did not normally coincide. They also knew that the briefing officers were themselves often uninformed—concerned, perhaps sometimes excessively, for military secrecy—and resentful of correspondents' badgering. . . .

Senior US officers did, of course, lie to make a case or extemporized when they did not know the answers. From those practices sprang the bitterness that corroded relations between the press and officialdom. No one likes to be treated as a fool even in the best of causes (and no one thought Indo-China was the best of causes). The military were in turn bitter at the unfairness they attributed to correspondents. . . .

Official deceit was thus exacerbated by incompetent journalism. While complaining about the press, many US officials, who knew they were fighting "a media war," sought to manipulate— rather than inform—correspondents. But they were not skilled at manipulation. While complaining about the government's duplicity, many editors assigned correspondents who were not qualified to fill a normal foreign post, much less to thread the labyrinthine complexities of the Indo-China War. Some editors told their correspondents what they wanted, while many correspondents had made up their own minds before they arrived "in country." Only a few, I trust, were in the unhappy position of the correspondent of an aggressively liberal US FM-radio station who, as he confided to me, was told: "Not *every* story has to be anti-war."

Beyond the pressure exerted upon them, most correspondents—serving six-month to two-year tours—were woefully ignorant of the setting of the conflict. Some strove diligently to remedy that crippling deficiency by reading widely and interviewing avidly. Many lacked the time or the inclination to do so—or any real awareness of how crippling their ignorance was to them professionally. Most, as I have noted, knew little about war in general from either experience or study—and less about the theory or practice of guerrilla war. They were untutored not only in the languages, but also in the history, culture, ethnography, and economics of Indo-China, let alone of China and Asia. Since so many were also untroubled by acquaintance with Marxist theory or practice and were hazy about the international balance of power, they were incapable of covering effectively a conflict involving all those elements. . . .

The atmosphere "in country" was heavily oppressive, as was our awareness that we were writing for a public that had virtually prejudged the War. My Lai was not reported at the time because the military effectively camouflaged that atrocity. Other allied excesses *were* reported; and Viet Cong atrocities were often discounted. Myths flourished because of the journalists' bias and the contempt they felt for the Vietnamese.

By innuendo and mis-statement [*sic*] the Army of the Republic of Viet Nam was reduced in the public eye to a corrupt rabble; far, far less effective than the Republic of Korea Army during the earlier war. In reality, the ARVN was strikingly more effective than the ROKA had been; but correspondents were friendly to the ROKA and antagonistic to the ARVN.

[One false but widely reported] tale of hundreds of Vietnamese soldiers bandaging non-existent wounds in order to be evacuated as casualties was just one example. That graphic and erroneous story reinforces the general impression that the cowardly South Vietnamese were unwilling to fight in defence of their own cause. That misleading conclusion undoubtedly encouraged US reluctance to supply Saigon's forces adequately after the American withdrawal. That reluctance, which contributed decisively to the final collapse, was then "proved" correct.

Despite their own numerous and grave faults, the South Vietnamese were, first and last, decisively defeated in Washington, New York, London, and Paris. Those media defeats made inevitable their subsequent defeat on the battlefield. Indo-China was not perhaps the first major conflict to be won by psychological warfare. But it was probably the first to be lost by psychological warfare conducted at such great physical distance from the actual fields of battle—and so far from the peoples whose fate was determined by the outcome of the conflict.

Once Again—Did the Press Lose Vietnam?
Charles Mohr

The ultimate failure (I have chosen that word with care—United States troops were never defeated militarily and, until very late in the war, no sizable South Vietnamese unit ever broke, was overrun, or defeated) of [the U.S. military engagement in Vietnam] became undeniable by April of 1975, when Saigon fell to North Vietnamese troops. So painful was the Vietnam experience that both the U.S. Army and civilians seemed to want to put Vietnam out of memory.

In the last few years, however, there has been a resurgence of interest in the war. A number of historical treatments and analytical discussions of the conflict have been published. Even a controversy about the design of the emotionally moving Vietnam memorial in Washington aroused controversy about the way the war was fought,

From Charles Mohr, "Once Again—Did the Press Lose Vietnam? A Veteran Correspondent Takes on the New Revisionists," *Columbia Journalism Review* (Nov/Dec 1983): 51-8. Reprinted with permission.

the way it was supported or obstructed by Congress and the public—
and the way it was reported by American journalists. . . .

Unfortunately, much of the discussion of the war has involved a
kind of revisionist "history" which, in fact, comes from people who
are not historians and who are not using historical methods. . . .

Notable among the critics, writing and speaking with varying degrees of bitterness and coherence, have been the editorial page of *The
Wall Street Journal*, Robert S. Elegant (a former *Los Angeles Times* reporter), William F. Buckley, John P. Roche, Walt W. Rostow, William
C. Westmoreland, Richard M. Nixon, and Henry A. Kissinger. This is
not meant to be a full list, nor do I intend to focus my rebuttal specifically on those I have named. . . .

Some of these critics have drawn conclusions that bear little relation to the actual conduct of mainstream journalists for major news
organizations in the years 1961 to 1975. Some of their conclusions
also reflect an astonishing misrepresentation, or at least misunder-
standing, of the nature of the war. This can be especially disturbing
when it comes from former civilian officials who helped to manage
and prosecute the war. There is also confusion about the manner in
which events actually unfolded, the problems of Vietnam war correspondence, and what the journalists *actually* said and wrote.

Although I like to argue that wars are not lost in the newspapers
(or in television broadcasts), the revisionist argument goes far towards
making that claim. In some cases it is flatly made. The core of the
complaint is complicated, and not always quite coherent. Although to
answer the critics it is necessary to discuss the entire course of the
war, it is also convenient to focus on Tet.

One element of the revisionist argument is that Tet was not only a
"victory" for the U.S.-South Vietnamese coalition, but that this was
clearly and unmistakably true, and that willful misrepresentation by
reporters caused a collapse of United States domestic morale in the
first days of the offensive.

Certainly, massive erosion both of domestic American public support for the war, and of public confidence in the country's policy-
makers, did eventually follow the Tet offensive. Such erosion was already well advanced among the members of the antiwar movement.
But in its magnitude, the loss of support among the general public
to some extent genuinely surprised me and a number of other "veteran" Vietnam war correspondents. The revisionists ascribe the erosion to hysterical reporting from Vietnam; my own belief is that it
was the result of strong public shock following the highly optimistic
public claims of progress by American officials in the fall of 1967. A
few journalists lost their composure, but most Vietnam correspondents did not. I and most others, even in the earliest hours of the of-

fensive, did not believe that the enemy was going to "win" a military victory, capture the Saigon post office, and bayonet us and then allied high command in our beds. No fair reading of the body of news stories produced in early 1968 will sustain that myth. . . .

As early as late 1961, when the great Homer Bigart arrived in Vietnam for *The New York Times*, a degree of tension developed between some officials and most of the then tiny press corps. These differences, however, were not over the "morality" of the war or the desirability of winning (a concept not easy to define, then or later). Essentially, the dispute involved optimism versus pessimism, growing out of conflicting views about the way the war was being prosecuted and about the viability of the South Vietnamese government in a revolutionary conflict.

This debate was not essentially, as some seem to believe, a quarrel between the press and U.S. officials in Vietnam. It was, rather, a quarrel between factions within the U.S. Mission. For the most part, field advisers closest to the action and to the Vietnamese took the pessimistic view. Some of the more senior officials in Saigon, who were reporting to Washington on the progress of the programs they were themselves administering, were publicly and persistently optimistic. The reporters quickly became aware of this dispute because brilliant younger field officials and officers, as exemplified by the late John Paul Vann, increasingly turned to the journalists. The reporters did not invent the somber information that sometimes appeared in their stories. Nor did they relentlessly emphasize it.

One of the persistent myths about Vietnam journalism is that the copy was deeply colored by ideology, that it was loaded with strong advocacy, and that it muffled the voice and views of officialdom. Again, this misrepresents the actual news product. Much of it was cautious and bland—probably, in retrospect, too bland. For practical reasons, journalists always reported the claims, appraisals, and statements of the senior officials who asserted that "progress" was being made. These stories almost always got prominent play. At many points in the war, progress *was* being made and many journalists could see and agree that this was taking place. Less often, and seldom in shrill tones, correspondents also reported the countervailing views of Americans who were eager to place greater pressure on the South Vietnamese for better management of their war. It is mostly the latter stories that the revisionists and embittered officials, now retired, seem to remember today.

There is also the persistent argument that, because of television, Vietnam "was the first war that came into people's living rooms" and that TV coverage caused a fatal revulsion for the war. Several aspects of this argument fascinate me. It is often advanced by pro-war people who suggest that "seeing" the war did not bother them, but that other Americans would not be expected to withstand such a shock to the emotions. It also seems to reflect how isolated and safe America has been for most of its history. Most wars literally, not merely photographically, go through people's living rooms. The awesome casualty lists of World War I, the London Blitz, the stark still photography of World War II have never seemed to me to be less psychologically important than Vietnam TV coverage.

Rereading the Tet coverage, I am struck by how much space and emphasis were given to claims of "victory" when they were made. But, as we shall see, officials spent much of that period not claiming victory, but warning of harder fighting and ominous enemy threats.

The most serious charge made by the revisionists, and one of the most frequently repeated, is that the Vietnam press corps failed to report an allied victory at Tet and, indeed, concealed its existence. There were, unquestionably, flaws in the purely military coverage; and not all of them were sins of omission. But in its raw form the charge does not seem to hold up.

I believe that Tet represented a serious *tactical* defeat for the Viet Cong and their North Vietnamese superiors. But this did not ultimately constitute a strategic victory for South Vietnam. That should be obvious. It is also argued that Tet shattered, nearly destroyed, the indigenous guerrillas and forced North Vietnam to continue the war with its own regular army troops. This was to a large extent true; but it was also what almost all serious journalists reported (though anyone who was around at the time of the 1973 "truce" quickly learned that there were still many Viet Cong in the countryside five years later).

In early January of 1969, I wrote a story, which was printed on the front page of the [*New York*] *Times*, that began: "After days of overoptimism, false starts, half-completed programs and lost opportunities, the allied forces in Vietnam appear to be making major progress against the enemy." The story also said that officials with reputations for intellectual honesty and skepticism "believe they see a drastic decline in the fighting quality and political abilities of the Viet Cong guerrillas and modest improvements in South Vietnamese and American prosecution of the war. Taken together, these may have broken the stalemate of previous years." (The story also contained plenty of qualifications and warnings that great problems persisted.)

Did the story come too late, as I suspect some revisionist would argue? Perhaps. But, although I was proud of my willingness to follow my reporting to any conclusions to which that reporting led, the real point today is that the story turned out to be essentially wrong. It appeared in print just before Nixon and Kissinger took office. They adopted a policy of "Vietnamization" of the war. And although the pace of American withdrawal seemed too slow to many people in this country, it seemed fatally rapid to some journalists in Vietnam. Then, in 1973, Kissinger signed a peace treaty that left some 140,000 regular North Vietnamese troops on South Vietnamese soil. Together, these steps guaranteed ultimate collapse. The stalemate of previous years was broken, but in an entirely different way. . . .

As both its practitioners and critics should recognize, journalism is an imperfect instrument. The Vietnam reporters were far from blameless. Some stateside editors and executives also failed, both early and late, to assign enough staffers, or any staffers, to the story. The Vietnam press corps was woefully short on language skills. . . . Many were not sophisticated militarily, and too many posed as ordnance experts, ready to pronounce on the caliber of an incoming shell.

Before and after Tet, the story did often tend to overwhelm the essentially conventional journalistic methods we employed. Much went unreported, although this may have been unavoidable in a sprawling nation of forty-four provinces and scores of allied divisions and brigades.

Granted that much went unreported, that factual errors were not rare, that sometimes we were too argumentative and skeptical (although much of the time we were far too gullible), that we spent too much time covering American troops and too little time with the South Vietnamese. Still, in a broad sense, the coverage seems sound in retrospect. Not only ultimately, but also at each major milestone of the war, the weight of serious reporting corresponds quite closely to the historical record. Revisionists seem to fault correspondents for distrusting the version of events propounded by the most optimistic senior officials in Vietnam. But what if the correspondents had believed that version and had been guided by it in carrying out their assignment? In that case, the reporters' reputations, which are not unblemished, would be irredeemably tarnished.

Questions for Discussion

1. Is there any merit to the claim that the American press undercut the war effort in Vietnam? Does the press bear any responsibility for the failure of the military in that conflict?

2. What is the proper role of the press in covering war? Is it possible to report in an unbiased way on something as emotionally charged as war?

3. Does bad news weaken the war effort? Is that the reporter's responsibility? What does the public have a right to know about military operations?

4. Journalism is often said to be the first draft of history. How can historians make sense of such a rough and controversial body of reporting? Is it a historian's job to judge the accuracy of the press?

13

The Cold War

Did Ronald Reagan
Win the Cold War?

On June 12, 1987, President Ronald Reagan stood in front of the Brandenburg Gate—one of the few portals in the wall that divided capitalist democratic West Berlin from communist East Berlin—and shouted, "Mr. Gorbachev, tear down this wall!" It was a dramatic moment in the long-running Cold War between the Western democracies, led by the United States, and the communist states of the Soviet Bloc. Mikhail Gorbachev, the Soviet premier, had already put in motion programs that were transforming the old Communist system to accommodate more individual initiative, but the end came with a flourish that few had expected. Little more than two years after Reagan's demanding speech, the Berlin Wall was torn down by Germans from both sides. Shortly thereafter, in 1990, the Russian economy collapsed catastrophically, signaling the death of the Communist experiment in Europe. Many commentators, including Dinesh D'Souza, who had worked in the Reagan administration, saw the Soviet crash as validation of the president's conservative policies, particularly his aggressive spending on military and defense programs. Other scholars like James Wm. Mooney believe that the greater share of credit belongs to the liberal politicians who charted the only reasonable response to Moscow's ambitions over the decades of the Cold War.

The strategy that the United States would pursue in the Cold War against the Soviet Union was outlined in 1946 by George Kennan, a State Department official whose "Long Telegram" from Moscow in 1946 and subsequent article, "The Sources of Soviet Conduct," published anonymously in *Foreign Affairs* the following year, argued that the Soviet regime was inherently expansionist and must be

136

strategically "contained" by the United States and its allies. In 1947, President Harry S Truman officially committed the United States to the policy of containment when he announced that the U.S. would send aid to countries threatened by totalitarian domination. The president did not name the enemy in what came to be known as the Truman Doctrine, but it was not hard to guess that he had the Soviet Union in mind, especially after the U.S. gave military and economic assistance to Greece and Turkey later that year to prevent Communists from establishing a foothold in those countries. The doctrine was a key tenet of U.S. foreign policy by the time Chinese Communists won control of their country in 1949, and when Korea threatened to follow suit the next year the American military led an international "police action" to prevent it.

Kennan soon claimed that his ideas had been misinterpreted, but the shape of the U.S. policy was set. Over the next four-and-a-half decades, the United States fought against the expansion of Communism with a combination of money, military aid, covert support of anticommunist forces, and open military engagement. The Cold War played itself out in the skies over Berlin, on the Korean Peninsula, in the warm seas off of Cuba, in the jungles of Vietnam, through the streets of Chile, on the tiny island of Grenada, and in other locales throughout the hemispheres, wherever strategic opportunities or threats were perceived. The world's two superpowers thrust and parried, each seeking to gain an advantage that would demonstrate the superiority of its ideology. At the outset of Ronald Reagan's presidency, it was uncertain who owned the upper hand, but by the time he left office the Soviet Union was clearly coming apart. Did Reagan's tough and instinctual stand against Communism reverse the tide against the USSR, or was he simply in the right place at the right time, benefiting from the policies of predecessors who had charted the course to victory over decades before Reagan took office?

How the East Was Won
Dinesh D'Souza

The man who got things right from the start was, at first glance, an unlikely statesman. He became the leader of the Free World with no experience in foreign policy. Some people thought he was a dan-

From Dinesh D'Souza, "How the East Was Won," *American History* 38, no. 4 (Oct. 2003): 37-43. Reprinted with permission.

gerous warmonger; others considered him a nice fellow but a bit of a bungler. Nevertheless, this California lightweight turned out to have as deep an understanding of communism as Alexander Solzhenitsyn. This rank amateur developed a complex, often counterintuitive strategy for dealing with the Soviet Union, which hardly anyone on his staff fully endorsed or even understood. Through a combination of vision, tenacity, patience and improvisational skill, he produced what Henry Kissinger termed "the most stunning diplomatic feat of the modern era." Or as Margaret Thatcher put it, "Reagan won the cold war without firing a shot."

Reagan had a much more sophisticated understanding of communism than either the hawks or the doves. In 1981 he told an audience at the University of Notre Dame: "The West won't contain communism. It will transcend communism. It will dismiss it as some bizarre chapter in human history whose last pages are even now being written." The next year, speaking to the British House of Commons, Reagan predicted that if the Western alliance remained strong it would produce a "march of freedom and democracy which will leave Marxism-Leninism on the ash heap of history.". . .

Appeasement, Reagan was convinced, would only increase the [Soviet] bear's appetite and invite further aggression. Thus he agreed with the anti-Communist strategy for dealing firmly with the Soviets. But he was more confident than most hawks in his belief that Americans were up to the challenge. "We must realize," he said in his first inaugural address, "that . . . no weapon in the arsenals of the world is so formidable as the will and moral courage of free men and women." What was most visionary about Reagan's view was that it rejected the assumption of Soviet immutability. At a time when no one else could, Reagan dared to imagine a world in which the Communist regime in the Soviet Union did not exist.

It is one thing to envision this happy state, and quite another to bring it about. The Soviet bear was in a ravenous mood when Reagan entered the White House. In the 1970s the Soviets had made rapid advances in Asia, Africa and South America, culminating with the invasion of Afghanistan in 1979. Moreover, the Soviet Union had built the most formidable nuclear arsenal in the world. The Warsaw Pact also had overwhelming superiority over NATO in its conventional forces. Finally, Moscow had recently deployed a new generation of intermediate-range missiles, the giant SS-20s, targeted at European cities.

Reagan did not merely react to these alarming events; he developed a broad counteroffensive strategy. He initiated a $1.5 trillion military buildup, the largest in American peacetime history, which was aimed at drawing the Soviets into an arms race he was convinced they could not win. He was also determined to lead the Western alliance in deploying 108 Pershing II and 464 Tomahawk cruise missiles in Europe to counter the SS-20s. At the same time, Reagan did not eschew arms control negotiations. Indeed, he suggested that for the first time the two superpowers drastically reduce their nuclear stockpiles. If the Soviets would withdraw their SS-20s, the United States would not proceed with the Pershing and Tomahawk deployments. This was called the "zero option."

Then there was the Reagan Doctrine, which involved military and material support for indigenous resistance movements struggling to overthrow Soviet-sponsored tyrannies. The administration supported such guerrillas in Afghanistan, Cambodia, Angola and Nicaragua. In addition, it worked with the Vatican and the international wing of the AFL-CIO to keep alive the Polish trade union Solidarity, despite a ruthless crackdown by General Wojciech Jaruzelski's regime. In 1983, U.S. troops invaded Grenada, ousting the Marxist government and holding free elections. Finally, in March 1983 Reagan announced the Strategic Defense Initiative (SDI), a new program to research and eventually deploy missile defenses that offered the promise, in Reagan's words, of "making nuclear weapons obsolete."

At every stage Reagan's counteroffensive strategy was denounced by the doves. The "nuclear freeze" movement became a potent political force in the early 1980s by exploiting public fears that Reagan's military buildup was leading the world closer to nuclear war. Reagan's zero option was dismissed by Strobe Talbott, who said it was "highly unrealistic" and offered "more to score propaganda points...than to win concessions from the Soviets." With the exception of support for the Afghan mujahedin, a cause that enjoyed bipartisan support, every other effort to aid anti-Communist rebels fighting to liberate their countries from Marxist, Soviet-backed regimes was resisted by doves in Congress and the media. SDI was denounced, in the words of *The New York Times*, as "a projection of fantasy into policy.". . .

The Soviet leadership, which initially dismissed Reagan's promise of rearmament as mere saber-rattling rhetoric, seems to have been stunned by the scale and pace of the Reagan military buildup. The Pershing and Tomahawk deployments were, to the Soviets, an unnerving demonstration of the unity and resolve of the Western alliance. Through the Reagan Doctrine, the United States had completely halted Soviet advances in the Third World—since Reagan assumed office, no more territory had fallen into Moscow's hands. Indeed, one small nation, Grenada, had moved back into the democratic camp. Thanks to Stinger missiles supplied by the United States, Afghanistan was rapidly becoming what the Soviets would themselves later call a "bleeding wound." Then there was Reagan's SDI program, which invited the Soviets into a new kind of arms race that they could scarcely afford, and one that they would probably lose. Clearly the Politburo saw that the momentum in the Cold War had dramatically shifted. After 1985, the Soviets seem to have decided to try something different.

It was Reagan, in other words, who seems to have been largely responsible for inducing a loss of nerve that caused Moscow to seek a new approach. Gorbachev's assignment was not merely to find a new way to deal with the country's economic problems but also to figure out how to cope with the empire's reversals abroad. . . .

Gorbachev was the first Soviet leader who came from the post-Stalin generation, the first to admit openly that the promises of Lenin were not being fulfilled. Reagan, like Margaret Thatcher, was quick to recognize that Gorbachev was different.

Even so, as they sat across the table in Geneva in November 1985, Reagan knew that Gorbachev would be a tough negotiator. Setting aside State Department briefing books full of diplomatic language, Reagan confronted Gorbachev directly. "What you are doing in Afghanistan in burning villages and killing children," he said. "It's genocide, and you are the one who has to stop it." At this point, according to aide Kenneth Adelman, who was present, Gorbachev looked at Reagan with a stunned expression, apparently because no one had talked to him this way before.

Reagan also threatened Gorbachev. "We won't stand by and let you maintain weapon superiority over us," he told him. "We can agree to reduce arms, or we can continue the arms race, which I think you know you can't win." The extent to which Gorbachev took Reagan's remarks to heart became obvious at the October 1986 Reykjavik summit. There Gorbachev astounded the arms control establishment in the West by accepting Reagan's zero option.

Yet Gorbachev had one condition, which he unveiled at the very end: The United States must agree not to deploy missile defenses. Reagan refused. The press immediately went on the attack. "Reagan-Gorbachev Summit Talks Collapse as Deadlock on SDI Wipes Out Other Gains," read the banner headline in *The Washington Post*. "Sunk by Star Wars," *Time*'s cover declared. To Reagan, however, SDI was more than a bargaining chip; it was a moral issue. In a televised statement from Reykjavik he said, "There was no way I could tell our people that their government would not protect them against nuclear destruction." Polls showed that most Americans supported him.

Reykjavik, Margaret Thatcher said, was the turning point in the Cold War. Finally Gorbachev realized that he had a choice: Continue a no-win arms race, which would utterly cripple the Soviet economy, or give up the struggle for global hegemony, establish peaceful relations with the West, and work to enable the Soviet economy to become prosperous like the Western economies. After Reykjavik, Gorbachev seemed to have settled on this latter course.

In December 1987, Gorbachev abandoned his previous "non-negotiable" demand that Reagan give up SDI and visited Washington, D.C., to sign the Intermediate Range Nuclear Forces (INF) Treaty. For the first time in history the two superpowers agreed to eliminate an entire class of nuclear weapons.

The hawks were suspicious from the outset. Gorbachev was a masterful chess player, they said; he might sacrifice a pawn, but only to gain an overall advantage. Howard Phillips of the Conservative Caucus even charged Reagan with "fronting as a useful idiot for Soviet propaganda." Yet these criticisms missed the larger current of events. Gorbachev wasn't sacrificing a pawn, he was giving up his bishops and his queen. The INF Treaty was in fact the first stage of Gorbachev's surrender in the Cold War.

Reagan knew that the Cold War was over when Gorbachev came to Washington. Gorbachev was a media celebrity in the United States, and the crowds cheered when he jumped out of his limousine and shook hands with people on the street. Reagan was out of the limelight, and it didn't seem to bother him. Asked by a reporter whether he felt overshadowed by Gorbachev, Reagan replied: "I don't resent his popularity. Good Lord, I once co-starred with Errol Flynn."

To appreciate Reagan's diplomatic acumen during this period, it is important to recall that he was pursuing his own distinctive course. Against the advice of the hawks, Reagan supported Gorbachev and his reforms. And when doves in the State Department implored Reagan to "reward" Gorbachev with economic concessions and trade benefits for announcing that Soviet troops would pull out of Afghanistan, Reagan refused. He did not want to restore the health of the sick bear. Rather, Reagan's goal was, as Gorbachev himself once joked, to lead the Soviet Union to the edge of the abyss and then induce it to take "one step forward."

This was the significance of Reagan's trip to the Brandenburg Gate on June 12, 1987, in which he demanded that Gorbachev prove that he was serious about openness by taking down the Berlin Wall. And in May 1988 Reagan stood beneath a giant white bust of Lenin at Moscow State University, where, in front of an audience of Russian students, he gave the most ringing defense of a free society ever offered in the Soviet Union. At the U.S. ambassador's residence, he assured a group of dissidents and "refuseniks" that the day of freedom was near. All of these measures were calibrated to force Gorbachev's hand.

First Gorbachev agreed to deep unilateral cuts in Soviet armed forces in Europe. Starting in May 1988, Soviet troops pulled out of Afghanistan, the first time the Soviets had voluntarily withdrawn from a puppet regime. Before long, Soviet and satellite troops were pulling out of Angola, Ethiopia and Cambodia. The race toward freedom began in Eastern Europe, and [in 1989] the Berlin Wall was indeed torn down. . . .

Finally the revolution made its way into the Soviet Union. Gorbachev, who had completely lost control of events, found himself ousted from power. The Soviet Union voted to abolish itself. Leningrad changed its name back to St. Petersburg. Republics such as Estonia, Latvia, Lithuania and Ukraine gained their independence.

Even some who had previously been skeptical of Reagan were forced to admit that his policies had been thoroughly vindicated. Reagan's old nemesis, Henry Kissinger, observed that while it was George H.W. Bush who presided over the final disintegration of the Soviet empire, "it was Ronald Reagan's presidency which marked the turning point."

Liberals and the Collapse of Communism
James Wm. Mooney

When the Soviet Union collapsed, along with the system of central and Eastern European nations that had become communist under Moscow's domination, historians started immediately to explain the reasons for an event that only a few years earlier would have been far outside prediction. Amid the diversity of possible causes, that closest in time could be defined as President Ronald Reagan's willingness to take seriously the good if self-interested intentions of Mikhail Gorbachev, the reformist general secretary of the Communist Party of the USSR and therefore in effect leader of the Soviet Union. When Reagan, to the dismay of the political right, went with his intuition rather than his hard-line anticommunist ideology, Gorbachev was given international credibility and stature as he pursued his policy of liberalization at home and peace abroad. And he needed all the credibility he could get, for his reforms faced the opposition of military and ideological forces deeply entrenched within the USSR. Gorbachev in turn was aided by the social and economic degeneration of the Communist system in its later years, which made reform necessary. Much of the credit for that degeneration should go to generations of dissidents within the USSR and its satellite states. Ultimately, the ending of the system came of the failures programmed into a mindlessly rigid, bureaucracy-clogged system from its beginnings.

But outside the Communist empire were forces that would contribute to the strains within it. There came the invasion by Nazi Ger-

Original contribution.

many, Moscow's cousin in genocide. And soon after the victory of the Allies, which then included the Soviet Union, in World War II, there came into existence another power that would more slowly, but relentlessly, ground down the Communist empire from without even as the USSR seemed to be at its greatest point of success. It was the coalition of anticommunist nations, once again using the name "Allies," that joined the North Atlantic Treaty Organization, initiated by the United States. NATO, coupled with a skilled combination of diplomacy and military force, was largely the work of Democratic and Republican liberals.

At the end of the Second World War, a good part of the Republican Party had turned back to the isolationism favored by conservatives before the nation entered the war. Objections on the part of isolationists repelled by Truman's policies lay in part in a dislike of any large international undertakings. Like President George W. Bush, they shunned entanglements with foreign countries. But while Bush avoids entanglements in his War on Terror by substituting dictation for cooperative diplomacy, postwar conservatives wanted the much more modest course of simply withdrawing from any major involvement in the troubles of the world outside our shores. We had, they reckoned, a navy and air force sufficient to protect us against Moscow. Whatever might be the fate of Europe was for Europeans to handle. That feeling went with a positive hostility toward Western Europe, which isolationists saw as weak and decadent. Then there was the conservative distaste for spending money for anybody's troubles. In the thirties Americans on the right had recoiled from new programs that taxed the propertied for the sake of the poor: Violation of property rights, they thought it. Now here we were, at it again, throwing away our wealth and energy, this time in the form of military and economic assistance to Western European nations.

At apparent opposites to this was the conviction among conservatives that Democratic liberals were weak on Communism. They despised the Truman Doctrine, the Marshall Plan, NATO, the Berlin Airlift, the whole range of policies taking dollars from American pockets to help somebody else. Those policies, their designers proclaimed, were for the containment of Communism. And as militantly anticommunist right-wingers saw it, containment amounted to cowardice: "appeasement," as they labeled it. Containment in the view of belligerent right-wingers allowed Communism to continue within its own borders, imposing suffering daily upon its imprisoned peoples of the Soviet Union, Moscow's Eastern European satellites, and China. And as it would do thereafter, the aggressively anticommunist right discerned as not far different from Communism the whole of socialism. As to how Communism was to be rolled back, extreme rightists had not a single suggestion. They did not call for sending troops smashing through Eastern Europe to Moscow and through China to Beijing. They had vague fantasies of sending aid to underground movements in communist countries, but not American soldiers. Within the unfocused angers on the conservative extreme, verbal anticommunist militancy mingled with the rhetoric of resentful isolationism, at times in the same individual.

Even as late as the Republican primaries of 1952, isolationism lived in the form of the candidacy of Senator Robert A. Taft, but the nomination of General Dwight D. Eisenhower confirmed Truman's internationalist course against the Communist powers. A policy of containment was to be replaced by a policy of liberation. But the moderate-to-liberal Republican presidency of Eisenhower kept to containment. It did back a coup that toppled a social democratic regime in Guatemala, which thereafter suffered from one regime after another of torture and murder. But the real tests of Eisenhower's administration came in the mid-fifties. At a Geneva summit in 1955 the leadership of the United States, Britain, and France met with that of the Soviet Union. There Eisenhower labored for a less confrontational relationship between the Communist and the Allied world, proposing an agreement on the part of each camp to allow planes from the other to fly over its opponent's territory and assure that no secret nuclear facilities were being built. Moscow rejected the idea. (Ronald Reagan, whose constituency wanted much to perceive the president as an uncompromising superhawk, would later make an offer similarly allowing each power to inspect the nuclear facilities of the other.) The next year the Hungarian premier Imre Nagy, a Communist opposed to Moscow's domination of his country, announced Hungary's independence of its overlord, and Soviet troops brutally crushed his rebellion. But Eisenhower again stuck with containment. He did not heed Nagy's call for Allied military intervention, choosing instead to accept a regional horror in Hungary over risking the global horror of nuclear war. The American far right, by now convinced that the Republican president was a crypto-liberal appeaser, offered no seriously dangerous countersolution.

During the late 1940s and the early 1950s the right had a plan for confronting Communism that was emotionally gratifying, politically inviting, and free of anything like military danger. Spurred in part by the policy begun in the Truman administration to clear Communists from the federal government, hardcore Democratic and Republican anticommunists pursued a program of rooting Reds out of government, the schools, libraries, Hollywood, or wherever else they suspected that subversives were lurking. Unlike the Soviet Union, a left-leaning librarian could not shoot back. Still another advantage was that in looking for Communists, right-wingers could pursue independent socialists and other radicals on the assumption that self-proclaimed progressives might be hidden Party members. They could even suggest that the New Deal had been soft on Communism out of secret sympathy with it. Communists, after all, believed in destroying private property; the New Deal scooped at least some bits of property out of the vaults of the prosperous classes; so therefore . . .

Heading the Red hunts was Wisconsin's Republican junior senator Joseph McCarthy, who beginning in 1950 made claim after claim of knowing the names of Communists hidden in the government. If publicly attacked, McCarthy would raise questions about the loyalty of his critic. Enjoying legislative immunity from libel suits so long as he made his accusations from the Senate floor, McCarthy was free to throw names around. Almost all Republicans allowed McCarthy to do his dirty work without criticism. Conservatives for whom steady, reasoned judgment and seasoned liberties meant something were appalled as, of course, were liberals, some of them targets of McCarthy's slanders. Eisenhower, though privately disgusted, lacked the taste for political dispute that might have drawn him into an open fight with McCarthy. In 1954 the Senate finally got up the courage to censure its embarrassing member for his behavior, and his fall into disgrace essentially ended the period of right-wing Red-baiting.

Liberals did their own baiting. They whispered—accurately, but it was none of their business—of homosexuality on McCarthy's staff. Toward the end of Eisenhower's second term they made another accusation, in this case sober but wholly inaccurate: They warned that under the placid Republican administration of the mild and unambitious Eisenhower, the country had fallen behind the Soviet Union in the production of nuclear missiles. The nation, they asserted, was becoming soft and lazy; at a time when scientific and technical advances made imperative a toughly schooled youth, education was insufficiently demanding of their brains and mental discipline; the country was stagnating in complacency while Communism gained strength abroad. The nation needed new energies, and the young Democratic senator John Kennedy of Massachusetts, a war hero who embodied vigor (his many illnesses were unknown to the public) and intellectual restlessness, could provide them. In 1960 Kennedy won the presidency against Eisenhower's vice president, Richard Nixon.

Kennedy restored to foreign policy much of the urgency it had possessed under Truman and then lost during the Eisenhower years. In 1961 he launched the unsuccessful invasion of Cuba at the Bay of Pigs planned by Eisenhower and enlisting anti-Castro exiles of both the right and the left pole of ideology. But he had the caution to refrain from sending in air strikes to support the rebel army as it floundered on the Cuban beach. In October of the next year came a critical moment in the Cold War, when upon discovering a buildup of

Soviet missiles in Cuba Kennedy set around the island a blockade, for which he used the milder term "boycott," against the shipment of further missile equipment from the USSR. After thirteen tense days while the world held its breath and the two superpowers privately negotiated, the Soviet premier Nikita Khrushchev agreed to dismantle the missiles in exchange for essentially minor concessions on the part of the United States. Thereafter there emerged a cautious friendship between Khrushchev and Kennedy.

In foreign policy, the Kennedy administration brimmed with fresh initiatives. A Peace Corps would enlist idealistic Americans in programs that sent them and their knowledge into impoverished regions needing teachers, mechanics, and other hard unglamorous skills. The Special Forces, or Green Berets, were to be both experts in small-scale antiinsurgent combat and experts in building good relations with communities wracked with guerrilla warfare: a sort of military twin to the civilian Peace Corps. Kennedy's Alliance for Progress aimed at giving economic aid to Latin American countries while it encouraged them to democratize their politics and society. He sought, in effect, what liberals had envisioned in their early days: a partnership between the United States and progressive anticommunist forces abroad.

The right had little to say or contribute. Conservative anticommunist militants had devoted their passions to domestic Red hunts. Foreign policy confused them. It took time for them even to recognize the significance of the break between Communist Moscow and Communist Beijing. It seemed to offend them, this unaccountable division within a theoretically indivisible ideological evil. The communist world had already split in 1948 when the dictator Josip Broz Tito of Yugoslavia defied Stalin's effort to control the Balkan republic. But a rupture as huge as the divorce between China and the USSR, a violation this deep of the American right's perception of the nature of Communism: It had to be denied or accounted away. Perhaps, a few conservative militants suggested, the whole business was a fake, designed to confuse the West. That, at least, would restore the ordered moral universe, cleanly setting a unified Communist evil against a unified capitalist good, that answered to the simplicities of their world vision.

On the big question of whether Kennedy would have taken the United States fully into the war in Vietnam, no answer can be anything other than speculative. His vice president Lyndon Johnson inherited the issue of Vietnam, and an alliance between the United States and South Vietnam that had begun under Eisenhower and accelerated in Kennedy's tenure turned into the massive involvement that Johnson entered in 1965.

It was an unwise act, and liberals were more equipped than conservatives to say why. For some time Kennedy and his associates had been recognizing the differences among Communist movements, along with the difference between Communism in general and other radical insurgencies against governments that repressed the poor. That ability to make distinctions and calculate policy on the basis of them is much of the reason that rightist hard-liners considered liberals soft on Communism. But in Vietnam, Johnson succumbed to the belief that communism was Communism and a triumph for North Vietnam and the Vietcong guerrillas would be a triumph for Vietnam's gigantic neighbor, China. Hanoi, in fact, looked more to the USSR than to China, which the Vietnamese distrusted as a threat to their independence.

Among the liberals who conducted the American engagement in Vietnam, some hoped for the establishment of a kind of social democracy. The fortified hamlets into which the Saigon government of South Vietnam, in its war with the Vietcong, drew peasant families: Why not make them experiments in a more equitable distribution of property and power? Saigon would have none of this kind of redistribution of power and wealth. Instead, the war continued to pit a corrupt and ineffectively repressive South Vietnamese regime against a strong and successfully repressive North Vietnam. The American presence merely multiplied the killing, until under the Republican presidency of Richard Nixon the United States came to see that propping up Saigon was hopeless.

The Nixon administration, installed in 1969 and actually liberal in domestic policy, did one thing that conservatives wanted to do: to combat not big Communist regimes but small leftist forces, whether Communist or not, which the political right detested for attacking capitalist property and privilege. Under Nixon, the CIA arranged a coup that overthrew the progressive government of Salvador Allende in Chile. There followed several years of torture and military rule. Nixon, together with his national security advisor and then secretary of state Henry Kissinger, also did something that conservatives disliked. He worked for better relations with both China and the Soviet Union. Containment of Communism would give way to pure considerations of Realpolitik. Power, in tenuous and wary peace with other powers whatever their ideology, was to govern the planet: capitalism in Western Europe and North America; Communism behind the Iron and the Bamboo Curtain; the military in Chile.

It was a liberal Democratic president, Jimmy Carter, who returned to the idea from which the Cold War had taken its shape. He knew, like everyone else with an ounce of intelligence, the massive moral distinction between democratic freedom and Communist totalitarianism. But he also believed that consistency demanded criticism of right-wing oppressive governments friendly to the United States. For such decisions as his refusal to support the Somoza regime in Nicaragua in its losing battle with Sandinista rebels, he gained the animosity of conservatives. Yet after the Soviet invasion of Afghanistan near the end of his presidency, he began the policy of aid to the anticommunist resistance (which, it turns out, contained elements more viciously repressive and more viciously fanatic than the communists) and cut off grain supplies to the USSR. Carter's human-rights policy was partial and not very effective, but it has been valuable in raising the consciousness of his country to the sins of torture regimes friendly to capitalism and to Washington.

In response to Carter, conservative intellectuals joined a revived Committee on the Present Danger, which had first formed early in the Cold War to heighten the public's awareness of the nature of the Communist threat. Disagreeing with official intelligence sources, the CPD insisted that the Soviet Union was increasing its strength relative to that of the United States. The committee members got it absolutely wrong; the USSR was crumbling of inefficiency. But it was great fun to imagine, in the comfort of their offices, that peril lurked somewhere outside and only the CPD knew of it. They welcomed the victory of Ronald Reagan in 1980. Now the country had been rescued from the Present Danger invited by what they thought to be the weakling Carter. And with Reagan's installation, Carter's half-formed policy of human rights gave way to a vigorous collaboration with Central American regimes notorious for torture and massacre.

To Reagan's massive increase in the country's military power conservatives attribute the fall of the Soviet Union. It imposed on the economy of the USSR, they concluded, unbearable strains as Moscow scrambled to keep up with the American war machine; and that forced reform of the unworkable Communist system, a reform that led to the disintegration of Communism itself. The argument is puzzling. How is it that a regime growing in relative power in the late 1970s, as the CPD insisted, could also be so frail as to collapse in a short-term economic competition with the United States? And why would dedicated Communists resolve to pursue a parity in strength with the West that they had never achieved and never could, and upon the failure of that project decide to stop being dedicated Communists and reform themselves to death? Conservatives in the 1980s enjoyed the kind of situation that their moral and intellectual inferiors, the Red-hunters of fifties, had momentarily attained. They could raise the military budget and posture toughness from a position of ease and safety. Reagan's genuine contribution to triumph in the Cold War was one thing conservatives did not want: When he was not posturing, he fell back to a simplicity and openness that allowed him to befriend Gorbachev.

So closed the last chapter in a continuing quarrel between liberalism and the right over the nature of international politics. For decades, liberal administrations had stubbornly and patiently with-stood Communism. They built alliances. When they could, they bar-gained with the enemy for enough peace to keep the world a little safer. When they thought it necessary, they went to war. At all times, they required of the nation enough of its treasure to sustain the nec-essary military and foreign aid. They passed the Marshall Plan and created NATO; they sent forth the Peace Corps; they fought in Korea and Vietnam. It was an unbearable strain on the nerves of conser-vative militants. They hated the taxation; they hated the restraints imposed by diplomatic alliances; above all, they hated the grim, per-sistent patience of liberal foreign policy. (Nixon and Kissinger, astute diplomats, tried to substitute power-sharing for confrontation: an ugly but relatively stable alternative to the Cold War at its angrier mo-ments.) Rightists wanted a more gratifying kind of anticommunism, stronger in its denunciations of the Communist evil. What they did not want is difficulty.

Here Reagan's administration was quick to satisfy them. The Re-publicans had no intention of putting their affluent American con-stituency through the slightest effort and pain. Their actions were dramatic, but essentially safe. Reaganites would not tax the public for the Cold War. Their strategy was to cut down on domestic programs, build up the military, and borrow the money. That way the prosper-ous classes could play at getting wealthier, and at no expense, while the administration played at being confrontational. And the human-rights policy of the Carter years, which required condemning repres-sion in rightist and leftist regimes alike, was far too demanding for the Republican ideological taste.

Communism, meanwhile, was expiring as it continued mechanically to speak the empty formulas of its ideology, until in relief, its leaders gave up the formulas and the ideology. The sober resistance of the West for four decades, the struggles by dissidents within Communist regimes, and finally the internal absurdity of Communism itself had defeated it.

Questions for Discussion

1. To what extent was Reagan's strategy responsible for the Soviet collapse? What role did earlier administrations play in the Cold War? Who deserves the most credit for the defeat of Commu-nism?

2. Ultimately, what was at stake in the Cold War? What did the Cold War victory mean for the United States? For the world?

14
After 9/11

A Brave New World?
How Should the United States
Conduct the War on Terror?

In his 2004 State of the Union address, just over two years after the September 11 terrorist attacks on the World Trade Center in New York City and the Pentagon in Washington, D.C., President George W. Bush surveyed the nation's response and found a "confident and strong" populace "rising to the tasks of history." He urged Americans to keep up the fight against terrorism by supporting the troops abroad and strengthening the economy at home. The historian Thomas West disagrees with this assessment of the nation's War on Terror and the president's prescription for winning it. While West acknowledges the disaster of 9/11 and the merit of removing Iraqi dictator Saddam Hussein from office, he questions the validity of the president's conduct, the wisdom of his agenda, and his commitment to the conservative and Christian foundations of the modern Republican Party. If President Bush and his critics agree on anything, it is that—for good or for ill—the nation's response to September 11 is charting a course that will resonate with tremendous implications for future generations.

President Bush responded to the 9/11 attacks by declaring war on terror, and in short order the United States opened battlefronts against the terrorists by invading Afghanistan and then Iraq. At home, Americans reflected on the reason for the attacks, on our relationship to the rest of the world, and on what it means to be the lone superpower in an age of terrorism. Many turned to history for perspective, pointing out that terrorism did not debut in the United States on September 11, 2001. It was not difficult to draw certain comparisons between suicide pilots like Mohammed Atta and John Brown, who had hoped to terrorize slaveholders and spark insurrection with his raid on Harper's Ferry in 1859, or Timothy McVeigh, who killed 168 people when he destroyed the federal building in Oklahoma City in 1995. Thoughtful commentators may have noted that the sinking of the *USS Maine* (probably not the work of terrorists or saboteurs, but widely interpreted as such at the time) in 1898 offered an opportunity to consider the media's role in shaping the American response. President Bush sees similarities between the fight against Islamic extremists and the Cold War struggle against communism. Thomas West views Bush's actions in the light of earlier abuses of presidential power, such as Franklin Roosevelt's plan to pack the Supreme Court with judges friendly to the New Deal.

In the days after 9/11 the president and his Republican allies enjoyed enormous popularity with American voters, which gave him virtually a free hand to shape foreign and domestic policy. Bush urged the passage of the USA Patriot Act, a bill aimed at strengthening the ability of law enforcement officials to prevent future terrorist attacks, and Congress overwhelmingly obliged. Bush also used his increased political capital to continue pushing for tax cuts, a staple of his economic philosophy, despite the heavy financial burdens of the War on Terror. Yet it seems that what goes up cannot help but come down, especially when the thing in question is political popularity. During the 2004 State of the Union address, members of Congress in the audience jeered when the president proposed making his tax cuts permanent. And in the years since the passage of the Patriot Act many Americans have grown concerned that the expanded powers granted to law enforcement officials infringe too far upon civil liberties.

George W. Bush is not the first American president to struggle with the balance between civil liberties and national security in a time of war. Abraham Lincoln suspended *habeas corpus* during the Civil War, Woodrow Wilson signed the Espionage and Sedition Acts during World War I, Franklin Roosevelt interned innocent Japanese American citizens during World War II, and numerous politicians fanned the hysterical flames of McCarthyism during the Cold War. President Bush has admirably distinguished himself from his predecessors by using his bully pulpit to warn Americans against thinking of Islam and its adherents as the enemy. But many Americans have become disillusioned with the Patriot Act's tradeoff of civil liberties for security, and the nation's claim to leadership in the world has been strained by the Bush administration's stark dictation of terms to its allies in the War on Terror.

In many ways, the American response to terrorism can be situated within the context of history, but historical comparisons should not overshadow the uniqueness of the moment confronting Americans. This book has examined events that shaped U.S. history and provoked passionate debate, among both observers at the time and generations of historians who followed. The War on Terror seems certain to join that list, and so makes an appropriate conclusion to this volume. Consider the major points of this debate, as the president and Thomas West have portrayed them. What lessons, if any, can the student of history apply to the challenges facing the United States today?

State of the Union Address
George W. Bush

January 20, 2004

We have faced serious challenges together, and now we face a choice: We can go forward with confidence and resolve, or we can turn back to the dangerous illusion that terrorists are not plotting and outlaw regimes are no threat to us. We can press on with economic growth, and reforms in education and Medicare, or we can turn back to old policies and old divisions.

We've not come all this way—through tragedy, and trial and war—only to falter and leave our work unfinished. Americans are rising to the tasks of history, and they expect the same from us. In their efforts, their enterprise, and their character, the American people are showing that the state of our union is confident and strong.

Our greatest responsibility is the active defense of the American people. Twenty-eight months have passed since September 11th, 2001—over two years without an attack on American soil. And it is tempting to believe that the danger is behind us. That hope is understandable, comforting—and false. The killing has continued in Bali, Jakarta, Casablanca, Riyadh, Mombasa, Jerusalem, Istanbul, and Baghdad. The terrorists continue to plot against America and the civilized world. And by our will and courage, this danger will be defeated.

From George W. Bush, "State of the Union Address" (Washington, DC: 2004), available at http://www.whitehouse.gov/news/releases/2004/01/20040120-7.html.

Inside the United States, where the war began, we must continue to give our homeland security and law enforcement personnel every tool they need to defend us. And one of those essential tools is the Patriot Act, which allows federal law enforcement to better share information, to track terrorists, to disrupt their cells, and to seize their assets. For years, we have used similar provisions to catch embezzlers and drug traffickers. If these methods are good for hunting criminals, they are even more important for hunting terrorists.

Key provisions of the Patriot Act are set to expire next year. The terrorist threat will not expire on that schedule. Our law enforcement needs this vital legislation to protect our citizens. You need to renew the Patriot Act.

America is on the offensive against the terrorists who started this war. Last March, Khalid Shaikh Mohammed, a mastermind of September the 11th, awoke to find himself in the custody of U.S. and Pakistani authorities. Last August the 11th brought the capture of the terrorist Hambali, who was a key player in the attack in Indonesia that killed over 200 people. We're tracking al Qaeda around the world, and nearly two-thirds of their known leaders have now been captured or killed. Thousands of very skilled and determined military personnel are on the manhunt, going after the remaining killers who hide in cities and caves, and one by one, we will bring these terrorists to justice.

As part of the offensive against terror, we are also confronting the regimes that harbor and support terrorists, and could supply them with nuclear, chemical or biological weapons. The United States and our allies are determined: We refuse to live in the shadow of this ultimate danger.

The first to see our determination were the Taliban, who made Afghanistan the primary training base of al Qaeda killers. As of this month, that country has a new constitution, guaranteeing free elections and full participation by women. Businesses are opening, health care centers are being established, and the boys and girls of Afghanistan are back in school. With the help from the new Afghan army, our coalition is leading aggressive raids against the surviving members of the Taliban and al Qaeda. The men and women of Afghanistan are building a nation that is free and proud and fighting terror—and America is honored to be their friend.

Since we last met in this chamber, combat forces of the United States, Great Britain, Australia, Poland and other countries enforced the demands of the United Nations, ended the rule of Saddam Hussein, and the people of Iraq are free.

Having broken the Baathist regime, we face a remnant of violent Saddam supporters. Men who ran away from our troops in battle are now dispersed and attack from the shadows. These killers, joined by foreign terrorists, are a serious, continuing danger. Yet we're making progress against them. The once all-powerful ruler of Iraq was found in a hole, and now sits in a prison cell. Of the top fifty-five officials of the former regime, we have captured or killed forty-five. Our forces are on the offensive, leading over 1,600 patrols a day and conducting an average of 180 raids a week. We are dealing with these thugs in Iraq, just as surely as we dealt with Saddam Hussein's evil regime.

The work of building a new Iraq is hard, and it is right. And America has always been willing to do what it takes for what is right. Last January, Iraq's only law was the whim of one brutal man. Today our coalition is working with the Iraqi Governing Council to draft a basic law, with a bill of rights. We're working with Iraqis and the United Nations to prepare for a transition to full Iraqi sovereignty by the end of June.

As democracy takes hold in Iraq, the enemies of freedom will do all in their power to spread violence and fear. They are trying to shake the will of our country and our friends, but the United States of America will never be intimidated by thugs and assassins. The killers will fail, and the Iraqi people will live in freedom. . . .

Because of American leadership and resolve, the world is changing for the better. Last month, the leader of Libya voluntarily pledged to disclose and dismantle all of his regime's weapons of mass destruction programs, including a uranium enrichment project for nuclear weapons. Colonel Qadhafi correctly judged that his country would be better off and far more secure without weapons of mass murder.

Nine months of intense negotiations involving the United States and Great Britain succeeded with Libya, while twelve years of diplomacy with Iraq did not. And one reason is clear: For diplomacy to be effective, words must be credible, and no one can now doubt the word of America.

Different threats require different strategies. Along with nations in the region, we're insisting that North Korea eliminate its nuclear program. America and the international community are demanding that Iran meet its commitments and not develop nuclear weapons. America is committed to keeping the world's most dangerous weapons out of the hands of the most dangerous regimes.

When I came to this rostrum on September the 20th, 2001, I brought the police shield of a fallen officer, my reminder of lives that ended, and a task that does not end. I gave to you and to all Americans my complete commitment to securing our country and defeating our enemies. And this pledge, given by one, has been kept by many.

You in the Congress have provided the resources for our defense, and cast the difficult votes of war and peace. Our closest allies have been unwavering. America's intelligence personnel and diplomats have been skilled and tireless. And the men and women of the American military—they have taken the hardest duty. We've seen their skill and their courage in armored charges and midnight raids, and lonely hours on faithful watch. We have seen the joy when they return, and felt the sorrow when one is lost. I've had the honor of meeting our servicemen and women at many posts, from the deck of a carrier in the Pacific to a mess hall in Baghdad.

Many of our troops are listening tonight. And I want you and your families to know: America is proud of you. And my administration, and this Congress, will give you the resources you need to fight and win the war on terror.

I know that some people question if America is really in a war at all. They view terrorism more as a crime, a problem to be solved mainly with law enforcement and indictments. After the World Trade Center was first attacked in 1993, some of the guilty were indicted and tried and convicted, and sent to prison. But the matter was not settled. The terrorists were still training and plotting in other nations, and drawing up more ambitious plans. After the chaos and carnage of September the 11th, it is not enough to serve our enemies with legal papers. The terrorists and their supporters declared war on the United States, and war is what they got.

Some in this chamber, and in our country, did not support the liberation of Iraq. Objections to war often come from principled motives. But let us be candid about the consequences of leaving Saddam Hussein in power. We're seeking all the facts. Already, the Kay Report identified dozens of weapons of mass destruction-related program activities and significant amounts of equipment that Iraq concealed from the United Nations. Had we failed to act, the dictator's weapons of mass destruction programs would continue to this day. Had we failed to act, Security Council resolutions on Iraq would have been revealed as empty threats, weakening the United Nations and encouraging defiance by dictators around the world. Iraq's torture chambers would still be filled with victims, terrified and innocent. The killing fields of Iraq—where hundreds of thousands of men and women and children vanished into the sands—would still be known only to the killers. For all who love freedom and peace, the world without Saddam Hussein's regime is a better and safer place.

Some critics have said our duties in Iraq must be internationalized. This particular criticism is hard to explain to our partners in Britain, Australia, Japan, South Korea, the Philippines, Thailand, Italy, Spain, Poland, Denmark, Hungary, Bulgaria, Ukraine, Romania, the Netherlands, Norway, El Salvador, and the seventeen other countries that have committed troops to Iraq. As we debate at home, we must never ignore the vital contributions of our international partners, or dismiss their sacrifices.

From the beginning, America has sought international support for our operations in Afghanistan and Iraq, and we have gained much support. There is a difference, however, between leading a coalition of many nations, and submitting to the objections of a few. America will never seek a permission slip to defend the security of our country.

We also hear doubts that democracy is a realistic goal for the greater Middle East, where freedom is rare. Yet it is mistaken, and condescending, to assume that whole cultures and great religions are incompatible with liberty and self-government. I believe that God has planted in every human heart the desire to live in freedom. And even when that desire is crushed by tyranny for decades, it will rise again.

As long as the Middle East remains a place of tyranny and despair and anger, it will continue to produce men and movements that threaten the safety of America and our friends. So America is pursuing a forward strategy of freedom in the greater Middle East. We will challenge the enemies of reform, confront the allies of terror, and expect a higher standard from our friends. To cut through the barriers of hateful propaganda, the Voice of America and other broadcast services are expanding their programming in Arabic and Persian—and soon, a new television service will begin providing reliable news and information across the region. I will send you a proposal to double the budget of the National Endowment for Democracy, and to focus its new work on the development of free elections, and free markets, free press, and free labor unions in the Middle East. And above all, we will finish the historic work of democracy in Afghanistan and Iraq, so those nations can light the way for others, and help transform a troubled part of the world.

America is a nation with a mission, and that mission comes from our most basic beliefs. We have no desire to dominate, no ambitions of empire. Our aim is a democratic peace—a peace founded upon the dignity and rights of every man and woman. America acts in this cause with friends and allies at our side, yet we understand our special calling: This great republic will lead the cause of freedom.

In the last three years, adversity has also revealed the fundamental strengths of the American economy. We have come through recession, and terrorist attack, and corporate scandals, and the uncertainties of war. And because you acted to stimulate our economy with tax relief, this economy is strong, and growing stronger.

You have doubled the child tax credit from $500 to $1,000, reduced the marriage penalty, begun to phase out the death tax, reduced taxes on capital gains and stock dividends, cut taxes on small businesses, and you have lowered taxes for every American who pays income taxes.

Americans took those dollars and put them to work, driving this economy forward. The pace of economic growth in the third quarter of 2003 was the fastest in nearly twenty years; new home construction, the highest in almost twenty years; home ownership rates, the highest ever. Manufacturing activity is increasing. Inflation is low. Interest rates are low. Exports are growing. Productivity is high, and jobs are on the rise.

These numbers confirm that the American people are using their money far better than government would have—and you were right to return it.

America's growing economy is also a changing economy. As technology transforms the way almost every job is done, America becomes more productive, and workers need new skills. Much of our job growth will be found in high-skilled fields like health care and biotechnology. So we must respond by helping more Americans gain the skills to find good jobs in our new economy. . . .

We must continue to pursue an aggressive, pro-growth economic agenda. Congress has some unfinished business on the issue of taxes. The tax reductions you passed are set to expire. Unless you act . . . the unfair tax on marriage will go back up. Unless you act, millions of families will be charged $300 more in federal taxes for every child. Unless you act, small businesses will pay higher taxes. Unless you act, the death tax will eventually come back to life. Unless you act, Americans face a tax increase. What Congress has given, the Congress should not take away. For the sake of job growth, the tax cuts you passed should be permanent.

Our agenda for jobs and growth must help small business owners and employees with relief from needless federal regulation, and protect them from junk and frivolous lawsuits.

Consumers and businesses need reliable supplies of energy to make our economy run—so I urge you to pass legislation to modernize our electricity system, promote conservation, and make America less dependent on foreign sources of energy.

My administration is promoting free and fair trade to open up new markets for America's entrepreneurs and manufacturers and farmers—to create jobs for American workers. Younger workers should have the opportunity to build a nest egg by saving part of their Social Security taxes in a personal retirement account. We should make the Social Security system a source of ownership for the American people. And we should limit the burden of government on this economy by acting as good stewards of taxpayers' dollars.

In two weeks, I will send you a budget that funds the war, protects the homeland, and meets important domestic needs, while limiting the growth in discretionary spending to less than 4 percent. This will require that Congress focus on priorities, cut wasteful spending, and be wise with the people's money. By doing so, we can cut the deficit in half over the next five years. . . .

We are living in a time of great change—in our world, in our economy, in science and medicine. Yet some things endure—courage and compassion, reverence and integrity, respect for differences of faith and race. The values we try to live by never change. And they are instilled in us by fundamental institutions, such as families and schools and religious congregations. These institutions, these unseen pillars of civilization, must remain strong in America, and we will defend them. We must stand with our families to help them raise healthy, responsible children. When it comes to helping children make right choices, there is work for all of us to do. . . .

For all Americans, the last three years have brought tests we did not ask for, and achievements shared by all. By our actions, we have shown what kind of nation we are. In grief, we have found the grace to go on. In challenge, we rediscovered the courage and daring of a free people. In victory, we have shown the noble aims and good heart of America. And having come this far, we sense that we live in a time set apart.

I've been witness to the character of the people of America, who have shown calm in times of danger, compassion for one another, and toughness for the long haul. All of us have been partners in a great enterprise. And even some of the youngest understand that we are living in historic times. Last month a girl in Lincoln, Rhode Island, sent me a letter. It began, "Dear George W. Bush. If there's anything you know, I, Ashley Pearson, age ten, can do to help anyone, please send me a letter and tell me what I can do to save our country." She added this P.S.: "If you can send a letter to the troops, please put, 'Ashley Pearson believes in you.'"

Tonight, Ashley, your message to our troops has just been conveyed. And, yes, you have some duties yourself. Study hard in school, listen to your mom or dad, help someone in need, and when you and your friends see a man or woman in uniform, say, "thank you." And, Ashley, while you do your part, all of us here in this great chamber will do our best to keep you and the rest of America safe and free.

My fellow citizens, we now move forward, with confidence and faith. Our nation is strong and steadfast. The cause we serve is right, because it is the cause of all mankind. The momentum of freedom in our world is unmistakable—and it is not carried forward by our power alone. We can trust in that greater power who guides the unfolding

of the years. And in all that is to come, we can know that His purposes are just and true.

May God continue to bless America.

Bush's War on the American Character
Thomas West

September 11, 2001, was a terrible day. It was so for the passen-
gers on the planes as they saw that their craft were about to smash
into the Twin Towers; and it was terrible for their friends and rela-
tives. For the United States as a whole, too, it was terrible.

But as disasters go, it was simply that: a disaster. Not nearly so
much so as the day in December 1860 when South Carolina began
the process of secession from the United States; and as a stain on the
nation's soul, not so much a disaster as the moment in the seventeenth century when indentured servitude turned into black slavery.
For people in Sudan facing rape, violence, and death; for the inhabitants of Chechnya in the midst of war; for Africans on their AIDS-
wracked continent; for much of the human race, terrible days are
commonplace. People make adjustments, make love, bear children,
and go about their daily business. And that, for the most part, is what
our fellow citizens did on September 11 and thereabouts. Think back
to that day and the days following, and you will probably remember
that amidst the shock and far more so the anger, you too went about
your business.

Americans, in short, acted as people do in bad times: soberly and
sensibly. But that is not as the president and the journalists described
them during those late summer and early autumn days, or as they
have described their compatriots since. Journalists outdid one another
in the shrillness with which they recorded what they thought to be
national panic. And as for President Bush: Aside from his admirable
call to his fellow citizens not to turn in hatred on Muslims, and aside
from his skillful handling of Afghanistan, he was determined to describe Americans as did the media. He spoke of crusades and insisted
on portraying Americans as terror-stricken. Alerts in various shades
of color-coding emanated from Washington. And within a couple of
years Bush was making war on Iraq, on the assumption that Americans have such a birthright to absolute safety and comfort that the
slightest possible danger against them—a danger, it turns out, for
which evidence had to be invented—justifies tearing a country to
pieces. It also turns out that the War on Terror justifies tax cuts for

Original contribution.

the wealthy, whose prudent investment will strengthen the economy against our foe. (Is there in the mind of the Bush administration anything, up to and including a solar eclipse, that doesn't argue for tax cuts?) The danger of terrorism demands raids on the environment in the form of oil drilling: To keep our economy vigorous we have to have extra fossil energy now, right now, never mind the depletion of sources for the future. Neither constitutional protections of personal liberty nor the nation's proud claim to disdain torture are worth keeping. The War on Terror is more important. So a cluster of Justice Department lawyers explain that as commander-in-chief, the president has plenary, unlimited power over prisoners. In the fear that the president insists has overtaken us, we need the safety that torture and domestic surveillance will give us; our frail sensibilities will accept nothing less.

It is a slander that the president—and for the sake of balance, it must be admitted, even more the press—have committed against a proud people, hard workers with steady nerves, and solid community activists. Well, possibly the contempt that all this invites from foreigners matters little. Despising Americans is good fun, and allows European and third-world intellectuals to compete with one another. But there are the practical considerations. For at least a year after 9/11 terrorists took joy in issuing warnings of what dreadful things they have in store for us. And who can blame them? Bullying the frightened schoolyard kid is a time-honored sport, and if the president and the media present us as frightened children, the temptation among terrorists to issue their blowhard threats must be irresistible. But who are the enemy anyway? Suicide bombings are a death cult, and a war against a death cult is about as bizarre as a war against Jim Jones or David Koresh. But it is convenient. Bush's rich get richer; contractors get rich exploiting third-world workers, skimming the Iraqis, and short-changing American soldiers, while other no-bid contracts go to construction businesses benefiting from disaster in New Orleans. And then may come the biggest benefit of all: a future given to the Republican Party, the wealthy, and the multinational corporations. Not everyone will gain, of course. But capitalism, with which Bush identifies the American dream, will gain enormously.

Not that the administration needed 9/11 to give it an ideology to live by.

Consider this exchange months before the terrorist attacks. In May 2001 Ari Fleischer, Bush's first press secretary at the White House, made clear the image of his country that Bush's presidency was willing to present to the world. "Does the President believe," asked a reporter, "that, given the amount of energy Americans consume per capita, how much it exceeds any other citizen in any other country in the world, . . . we need to correct our lifestyles to address the energy problem?" Fleischer responded with "a big no. The President believes that it's an American way of life, and that it should be the goal of policy makers to protect the American way of life. The American way of life is a blessed one." Fleischer's response bespeaks a wider notion on the part of the present administration: No demands are to be made on Americans that would diminish the comforts and luxuries and safety of their Blessed Way of Life.

Or consider this, just after the terrorist attacks. Did Bush propose even that tax cuts might be delayed to help pay for the war? Not a bit of it. Given another opportunity to define the American culture according to the president's perception of it, he urged his fellow citizens to prop up the economy by buying things. There was a time when Bush's compatriots prided themselves as workers, demanding of themselves that they practice the advanced knowledge of technology. That was a vision of the Kennedy and the Johnson administrations when they sought to retrain jobless Americans in the new skills of an evolving economy. But Bush had a different vision. Go be consumers: Do what Americans are good at.

Then came Iraq. Removing Saddam was a noble enterprise, and insofar as Bush believed in it, he deserves respect. But what has he allowed the project to become? One report has it that third-world workers lured to Iraq by big contractors are so wretchedly fed that some American workers out of simple decency have slipped food to their exploited fellow employees. Iraq is now a windfall for American and European entrepreneurs.

Well, then, maybe Bush has made the country safe for constitutional and moral conservatism. How exactly has he done that?

Conservatives insist on standing for the strictest interpretation of the Constitution. Bush's lawyers have written elaborate statements demonstrating that as long as he acts in his office of commander-in-chief, his powers know no limitation. By what interpretation of constitutional conservatism could that assertion possibly stand? The lawyers have also proclaimed that any congressional act limiting Bush's governance of the armed forces is an infringement by one branch of government on the authority of another. Yet Section 8 of Article 1 of the Constitution declares, among its many provisions, that "The Congress shall have Power . . . To make Rules for the Government and Regulation of the land and naval forces," and the Uniform Code of Military Justice, which contains provision against cruelty toward prisoners, is congressional law.

Conservatives during the administration of FDR were especially disturbed at the growth of presidential power. They rejoiced in the Supreme Court decision in the *Schechter* case, decided in 1935, finding that the National Industrial Recovery Act had unconstitutionally delegated to the president law-making powers reserved to Congress. They recoiled, with reason, from Roosevelt's effort to increase the number of Supreme Court justices, which would have allowed him to appoint more judges favorable to his view of the Constitution. The more recent elections of conservatives to the presidency, of course, have softened the conservative hostility to the power of the White House, but their older insight, that an overgrown executive branch threatens liberty and the Constitution, remains sound. That Bush's admirers ascribe to the commander-in-chief the authority to abuse enemy prisoners suggests that their conservative predecessors of the New Deal era were onto something worth worrying about. The only difference is that FDR, power-hungry though he was, also had the stature of a statesmanlike leader.

For much of the twentieth century, conservatives demanded strict limitation of the federal budget. In large part, they were wrong: Deficit spending allowed the government to enact programs for the public good. And at any rate their abhorrence of spending reflected their loathing of progressive taxation: notably insofar as it would make demands on the wealthy, which sooner or later deficit spending would require. But right or wrong, condemnation of debt-ridden government was conservative orthodoxy. The Bush presidency retains the conservative revulsion at progressive taxation of the rich, but as for deficit spending, his contempt for balanced budgets is boundless.

Then there is Bush's increasingly insistent embrace of evangelical Christianity. This is a new turn within conservatism. Evangelicals and other dedicated Christians have probably been on every side of every major issue in our country's history. But a hard-edged Christianity founded in rigorous obedience to Scripture energized the antislavery movement; it sent John Brown on his mad holy mission to inspire a slave rebellion; it fueled resistance to war; it energized the civil-rights movement; and whatever be the merits of the anti-abortion forces, among them as defenders of life are Christians who also rejected the conflict in Vietnam along with the death penalty. How does Bush's evangelical faith measure up?

Until recently, when Bush decided out of necessity to urge Americans to drive less, he was an enthusiast for capitalist petroleum gobbling—recall his press secretary's proclaiming, on the matter, that "the American way of life is a blessed one"—and he is still an enthusiast of capitalist wealth-making. Capitalism in its present expression, deprived of the moral austerity that accompanied the ethos of capitalism as well as socialism of a century ago, means unbridled buying of luxuries along with reasoned buying of necessities. Las Vegas is its

Rome, its Jerusalem, its Mecca. So evangelical severity is compatible with capitalist consumerism?

Or consider the Gospel command to the wealthy youth to give all he has to the poor. It is, to be sure, an imperative upon the conscience, and does not recommend a governmental program. But Bush's forces think that Gospel imperatives can be turned into governmental programs. So a governmental program as well suited to the Gospels as possible would go something like this: Tax away wealth and luxury and distribute to the poor. Perhaps bad economics, and perhaps bad Gospel, but it does answer as closely to the purpose as any federal project could. What would Bush's administrators think of the idea? Need that be asked?

At least it might have been expected of the administration that, for good or for ill, it would make the country safe for conservatism. Is conservatism too a victim of 9/11?

Questions for Discussion

1. What is the appropriate balance between civil liberties and national security? Are the two necessarily opposed?

2. Are President Bush's actions in the War on Terror consistent with the decisions of earlier wartime presidents? If so, does that mean they are justified?

3. What is the role of the media in shaping the nation's response to the War on Terror?

4. Does history provide useful examples to consider in shaping the nation's response to twenty-first-century terrorist threats? Are historians specially qualified to evaluate current situations? How do you think the historians of generations to come will evaluate the War on Terror?